The Lost Keys

The Lost Keys

Unlock the Secrets to Happiness

CHRIS SMITH

BALBOA PRESS

A DIVISION OF HAY HOUSE

Copyright © 2013 Chris Smith.

All rights reserved. No part of this book may be used or reproduced by any means, graphic, electronic, or mechanical, including photocopying, recording, taping or by any information storage retrieval system without the written permission of the publisher except in the case of brief quotations embodied in critical articles and reviews.

Balboa Press books may be ordered through booksellers or by contacting:

Balboa Press
A Division of Hay House
1663 Liberty Drive
Bloomington, IN 47403
www.balboapress.com
1-(877) 407-4847

Because of the dynamic nature of the Internet, any web addresses or links contained in this book may have changed since publication and may no longer be valid. The views expressed in this work are solely those of the author and do not necessarily reflect the views of the publisher, and the publisher hereby disclaims any responsibility for them.

The author of this book does not dispense medical advice or prescribe the use of any technique as a form of treatment for physical, emotional, or medical problems without the advice of a physician, either directly or indirectly. The intent of the author is only to offer information of a general nature to help you in your quest for emotional and spiritual well-being. In the event you use any of the information in this book for yourself, which is your constitutional right, the author and the publisher assume no responsibility for your actions.

Any people depicted in stock imagery provided by Thinkstock are models, and such images are being used for illustrative purposes only. Certain stock imagery © Thinkstock.

Printed in the United States of America

ISBN: 978-1-4525-6623-8 (sc)
ISBN: 978-1-4525-6624-5 (e)

Balboa Press rev. date: 09/23/2013

Contents

Introduction . . . . *xi*

FYI . . . . *xv*

Chapter - 1 Part 1
My Journey – Past Experiences 1

Chapter - 1 Part 2
Don't Worry Be Happy – Past Experiences. . . . 21

Chapter - 2
More To Life Than Working 9-5 – Spirituality. . 31

Chapter - 3
Kick Me When I am Down –
Setbacks & Expectations. 45

Chapter - 4
High as a Kite – Man's Vices. 59

Chapter - 5 Part 1
Second by Second – Living in the Present 73

Chapter - 5 Part 2
  Mother Nature & You Time – Living
  in the Present. 79

Chapter - 6
  Chilling & Zoning Out – Meditating 89

Chapter - 7
  SOS – Saving Our Planet 107

Chapter - 8 Part 1
  What You Give Out You Get Back – Karma . . .115

Chapter - 8 Part 2
  Compassion vs Terrorism – Karma 123

Chapter - 9
  Rabbit Food – Diet & Killing of Animals. 131

Chapter - 10
  Choose Your Future – The Power to Change. . .145

Chapter - 11
  Coming Out – Being You 155

Chapter - 12 Part 1
  Invisible Power – Love. 163

Chapter - 12 Part 2
  Compassion and Co-existence – Love 173

Chapter - 12 Part 3
  Relationships & Their Ups and Downs – Love. .183

Chapter - 12 Part 4
  Family Life & The Importance of You – Love . .193

Chapter - 12 Part 5
  The Power of Music & Conclusion
  of The Fifth Element – Love 201

Chapter - 13
    Six Feet Under- Death 209

Chapter - 14 Part 1
    No Such Thing as an Illness – The
    Power of The Mind. 229

Chapter - 14 Part 2
    The Power of The Mind – Mind Over Matter . 239

Chapter - 15
    Wise Up To The Real Reality –
    Putting Things Into Perspective. 245

Chapter - 16
    The Devil Within – Anger 257

Chapter - 17
    Underused Senses & Moving
    Forward – Senses & Our Future 263

Chapter - 18
    The Unlocked Doors – Conclusion
    of The Lost Keys 273

Acknowledgements 281

Introduction

We all know the secrets to happiness, as did the generations before us, but the difficult part is remembering how to access and use this Universal knowledge. The Lost Keys will show you the truth about the meaning and purpose of life, and how to deal with the ups and downs of living in our modern world.

You are one of the growing number of people who have realised there is more to the world we inhabit, a world where a **deeper meaning** exists that replaces scientific knowledge and, to some extent, traditional religious teachings. This life of uncertainty, confusion, and falsity needs to end now. You are reading this because on some level you have listened to your spiritual instincts and are aware of the dawning of a New Age, a dawning of new mindsets and values. In a world where science can no longer answer all of our questions about life and existence, you, and countless others are awakening to the realisation that life on Earth is not as it was intended to be lived, and a dramatic shift in consciousness is needed to correct it.

Wars that ravage human lives and environments, famines that kill thousands every day, destruction of whole cultures, dictatorships, infringement of basic human rights, poverty, global warming that has the ability to kill every single living species on this planet, murder of innocent people in the name of religion, rape, theft, animal cruelty, and pollution. Humanity has been out of control for far too long and unless we all come together as a **United World**, we will destroy our beautiful planet, and ourselves, forever.

NOW is the time for change. More people than ever before, at this moment in time are aware of the need for change and that is what makes this decade different from the revolutions and movements of the past.

We have had the age of Religion, the age of Science and materialism, and what awaits us now is the age of the New Consciousness. New mindsets and outlooks are needed so we can all become happier, more in-touch human beings. The New Age, which has been talked about for so long is actually here. A positive age of positive feelings, experiences, and actions. The best way to begin something new is by the complete destruction of the old. The New Age is doing just that, rising-up from the devastation we have caused to this planet, and from the turmoil experienced by individuals. We can all be part of this movement, regardless of who we are or where we are from.

By learning the true meaning of life, and our purpose, we can change ourselves for the better and, in turn, change the world for the better.

After reading The Lost Keys your outlook on life will never be the same again. So if you are not ready for this change, put this down and come back to it when you are. You don't have to believe in psychic or new age practices to get something from the Lost Keys, but it will help if you can read it with an open mind, and more importantly, relate the contents to your own life and personal journey.

Please suggest The Lost Keys to all your friends and relatives. I hope it helps with the many problems and issues we all share in life. If it only improves one aspect of your life then I have achieved my goal. Treat happiness like a relay. Pass the baton onto the next person; giving them what they need in order to run their leg of the race.

With this in mind, consider each chapter as a Lost Key that will help you unlock the secrets to happiness.

FYI

You will notice a ♪ symbol and then a song title underneath each chapter. I felt that as movies have soundtracks there was no reason why my book shouldn't have one too. These songs help me remember the keys to happiness and I hope they add something a bit different to your read. Soundtrack not included, so feel free to grab them from You Tube as and when you can.

Part 1

My Journey – Past Experiences

♪ Hometown Glory, Adele ♪

WHY DIDN'T SCHOOL TEACH US the most basic lesson of all? – "That life won't always be easy, it has ups and downs, and will be one big test" That would have made my life so much easier. Instead, I had to discover that lesson by myself, the hard way, but then I suppose we all do. Either way, it rather nicely starts my book, and sums up one of the main messages I want to share with you so you can lead a happier and more in-touch life. No one ever said life would be easy or full of happy experiences and laughter, it is just something we have come to expect, probably through exposure to the happily-ever-after books and movies of our youth. I am an optimist, and certainly don't believe expecting the worst to avoid disappointment. After much introspection and keeping my eyes and ears open I learnt that shit does, and will happen to all of us. It is how we deal with it, and more importantly, what we learn from it that makes us happy or sad. On that note I will get this show on the road and start sharing some of my life with you, and the lessons I learnt along the way that made me both happy and spiritual. I think these lessons are universal and apply to everyone. They are what I like to call The Lost Keys to happiness.

My close and loving family consists of my amazing single parent Mum, little sister Laura, older sister Vicki and older brother Simon. At fifteen I was delighted to discover we had another sister called Rachel, who had been adopted from birth as Mum was very young when she had her. I also got a fun nephew (Adam) and great brother-in-law (Dave) out of the surprise. My Gran and Grandpa were always on the scene, as were my Aunty Jan, Uncle John and only cousin Alex, who was like a little brother to me. We were raised traditionally, learnt manners from a young age, were not allowed to leave the table until we had eaten all our food, and we had to help with household chores – mainly because Mum couldn't do everything! I was taught ladies first, and I still can't walk through a door before the fairer sex. We were always busy doing something and I was usually roped into moving the furniture or mowing the lawns. God forbid, if we said we were bored, a list as long as Mum's arm would appear. My Mum and Dad got divorced when I was about six, and I can't remember anything about him. He didn't stay in touch after the divorce, and as you will find out, that was probably for the best.

My spiritual journey began from a young age. I was raised in a very 'New Age and Spiritual' environment, and was lucky enough to have been given a head start discovering the truths of the Universe. I don't mean a hippy or dope-smoking environment where we would chant under the moonlight and wear tie-dyed clothes. It was more "normal" – and I use the term loosely – than that! I grew up in a large family with my single parent Mum who, for as long as I can remember, has been interested in all things spiritual. I was a quiet, shy and inquisitive child, unnaturally sensitive to everything around me. At ten years old I found myself crying while watching one of those Oxfam sponsorship adverts, and as a result donated a pound from my meager monthly pocket money to help the cause. When we drove past old people crossing the road in pain, I would often find myself crying in the back of the car.

I found it difficult to sleep at night as my mind was a constant swirl of confusion about the world I lived in, the vibes I sensed from people, and the things I would see on TV. I would instantly pick up and feel other people's emotions and feel their pain, sadness and joy. I also had a chronic case of glandular fever leading to depression around the same time. Looking back I think I felt like this because I was absorbing all of the negative emotions and feelings I was subjected to back in the 90s.

I was absorbing these emotions and getting consumed by them due to my sensitive and antenna-like nature. I couldn't get to grips with the enormity of the situation – that situation being little Chris, plonked in a confusing, vast and hurtful world. I quite literally felt like an alien at times. However, help was at hand in the form of my loving, unique and special Mum.

As I began mixing with my classmates in the early years at school I realised my Mum wasn't as "typical" as I had first thought. I found myself embarrassed to invite friends over to my house in case they thought she was in need of urgent psychiatric treatment. A couple of my friends thought she was a Witch, and at the impressionable age of eight I decided it was best I went to their house to play, rather than face the ridicule and jokes at school the next day after a night at the Witches Lair!

My Mum's first love has always been crystals and their healing properties. She also follows the Buddhist way of life. Over the years she added all sorts of alternative medicine and psychic activities to her portfolio. These include hypnotherapy, spiritual healing, absent healing, colour therapy, reflexology, regression, aromatherapy, aura soma, dowsing, using pendulums and psychic readings to name but a few. Her crystal collection is still colossal. The surfaces in our house were covered in shiny light reflecting rocks and gems of all colours, shapes, and sizes.

In those days, as a quiet blonde-haired, blue-eyed kid, the crystals held a special power over me that captured my imagination. I would look into them and see whole universes swirling within their magical walls.

Without realising at the time, this was probably my first experience of meditation. I found that some crystals stood out more than others, they would call out to me by becoming more vibrant and lucid than their surrounding 'friends'. We would also dowse in the garden to find hidden objects, hug trees with my Mum's friends (didn't everyone?!), cleanse crystals, and experience all kinds of magical, exciting and soul stirring New Age activities. These types of experiences helped me adapt and deal with my very sensitive nature, and finally helped me to sleep peacefully and not absorb so much of the negative aspects of the world back in the late 80's and early 90's.

I grew up with hundreds of strangers coming in and out of our house, and this hasn't changed when I go back to visit now. The house seems to attract people like moths to a flame. Most of the visitors had heard through the grapevine that Mum could heal illness and was a great source of advice and comfort. I have seen rich businessmen, the terminally ill, possessed teenagers, alcoholics, drug-addicts, schizophrenics, and homeless people revolve through our front door. On the very rare occasions Mum was unable to cure them, they left as more relaxed and pain free people than when they arrived. Most would comment on the warmth they experienced as soon as they entered our house. "I feel safe and cradled here" I remember one of them saying as I was staring at the clouds of ever-present burning incense.

Simon and Vicki (my older brother and sister) would have their teenage friends over to our house regularly, and most of the time their friends would sit with my

Mum for hours discussing their problems about school or home life. I found it really weird to think they'd rather sit with my Mum than Vicky or Simon, but gradually, over time, I realised they felt comfortable talking to her about anything. They felt able to share their problems, and were receiving good advice in return without being judged. It finally clicked in my head that she was helping people in her own way, and I no longer had anything to be embarrassed about.

Twice a year Mum would hold a crystal-healing workshop in our adjoining converted barn. I would potter over to the barn during their lunch break (barely tall enough to open the rickety barn door) so I could eat some of the buffet food from under the table – I had a deep love for the canapés and am still very partial! I will forever have this image of her ingrained in my memory from my viewpoint under the tablecloth – Mum was standing in her long, free-flowing mauve gown, holding crystals in her hands with whale and dolphin music playing in the background. She was healing a person who was lying down on the long massage bed. All of this took place in front of a backdrop of silken drapes and her awe inspired class. She looked magical, powerful, and at the same time so very peaceful, in control, and positively flowing with love and a form of energy. She resembled some kind of Goddess or high priestess from early history and it simply blew my mind, and I can still remember thinking, "wow, that's my Mummy up there".

As I grew older and more aware of the good deeds she was doing, my little sister Laura and I used to sneak to the bottom of the stairs after we were put to bed to listen to the "readings" and feedback she would give to her 'clients'. That sounds like she was a prostitute, she wasn't, honest.

There was one person in particular that I will never forget. I don't know if I can put her real name in this book for fear of being sued, so for arguments sake lets call her Danielle. Danielle had manic depression, tried killing herself several times, was in and out of psychiatric hospitals, taking drugs, violent, and generally very unhappy with her life. A friend of the family suggested that she visit my Mum for a course of healing. Before Mum had chance to start the session, she received an urgent call from Danielle, who had her Doctor with her as she was suffering a "manic" stage, and he had organised for her to go into a nearby psychiatric unit. Danielle begged Mum to help her and the Doctor reluctantly agreed for her to stay with us, on the proviso he called in twice a day to check on her at our house. He was amazed when he visited later that day to find Danielle sleeping peacefully. She stayed with us for two weeks.

One night as Laura and I were crouching on the bottom step I remember overhearing a conversation that Mum was having with the friend who had introduced Danielle. Mum was saying that she felt an immense black cloud surrounding Danielle, and had an overwhelming sense that she was possessed by someone, or something else. Much coaxing later, Danielle finally admitted that she had dabbled in black magic and had been given a rag voodoo doll. If you do not believe in such things at this point, as I myself am unsure about ghosts and voodoo practices, keep an open mind and read on before making a judgment. Mum spoke to a priest, having researched exorcism and voodoo dolls, and then asked Danielle for the doll so it could be destroyed by fire. Laura and I were at school when this happened, but Mum told us later that the doll, made from rags, would not burn on the bonfire despite trying for five long hours. She and three other psychic friends tried petrol and firelighters but the thing did not burn as it should have. Vicky (older Sis) and some of the other villagers (this is beginning to sound like a plot from a horror movie!) can vouch for this as they were watching it unnaturally resist the flames that engulfed it. Its limbs jumped and moved and apparently it literally screamed before it was finally reduced to ashes that then had to be taken to consecrated ground! Three weeks passed after Danielle's exorcism, healings, and the burning of the doll without any word from her. Then the friend who had made the introduction got back in touch and told Mum that Danielle was a new person – happy, joyful, with a stable job, and enjoying life once again.

We saw Danielle once more when she returned to thank my Mum, and there was an unmistakable difference. She was no longer the demonic looking woman who Laura and I used to hide from; she looked refreshed, happy and kind-hearted. Something had changed *within* her, and I saw this transformation as a young and impressionable kid. It was visible in her mannerisms, personality and face – the black cloud had lifted. Whatever happened during her time with us changed Danielle's life for the better, and in my eyes my Mum was the reason for that positive transformation. These types of experiences enriched and influenced my childhood in a way I could not have predicted, but how quickly and easily we forget both the good and mysterious times of our youth.

In more recent years my Mum has given very successful psychic readings to friends of mine, friends of friends, and strangers. The advice she gives, via what she calls 'Spirit', brings up past issues that are affecting people and often making them physically ill. The realisation, once faced, enables them to overcome obstacles and move forward.

We were very broke throughout much of my childhood, I hadn't realised how bad it was until I asked Mum recently how she survived with four kids and no job. She said she remembers the worst times when she went without lunch and dinner to make sure we had enough. I cried when she told me this, it was such a shock and done in a way to shield us from knowing how bad things actually were. I do remember that Gran and Grandpa came over every Thursday with fresh fruit and vegetables. I suppose it didn't clock that we literally survived on this plus what little dried goods Mum managed to buy with her benefits. For some strange reason I always remember being envious of my friends who had microwave meals, we always had fresh food and lots of pasta, now I release its because we couldn't afford much else. We never had chocolate, and the few times we had crisps in the house they were supermarket's own brand and so thin they were a waste of time! When the Rees family moved into one of the largest houses for miles around, a boy called Nathaniel and I decided to introduce ourselves and have a nose around.

Luckily for me they had a son called Thom of the same age as me. We all hit it off and Thom and I have stayed friends to this day. I will always remember the "snack cupboard" at Thom's house, it was stuffed full of everything a deprived boy could have dreamed of. Crisps so thick you could get full from one bag, chocolate of every make and size, and biscuits with a million coatings. Thom used to let me sit in front of that snack cupboard and gorge like a refugee who hadn't seen food for months. Happy days! I soon tired of snack food and I am now not a fan, but in those days it was such a treat. Thom and I, plus many others who came and went over the years, had so much fun in Riseley – our little village in the middle of nowhere. We moaned about it, and dreamt of moving to London where the Rees's had just come from.

We always knew we were destined for the big city, but for the time being we made the most of village life, making crop circles with a rug as we had seen on "Strange But True".

We made 'secret' bases at a farmer's wood which had a beautiful trickling stream, and we called it JPSB (Jurassic Park Secret Base for those not in the gang!).

Thom and I liked being creative and instead of playing football like the other boys we preferred decorating our bedrooms like Harmony Granger's from the TV programme "The Queen's Nose". His room was above their garage in another wing of the house, so it lent itself rather nicely to our antics and allowed for more privacy than mine.

One day, in this annex, I decided I wanted a husky voice so I tried my first cigarette. I promptly vomited all over Thom's purple inflatable chair after my first drag. We snuck it down and put the chair in the wheelie bin and thought it would be the end of that experiment. Alas, Sandra, Thom's Mum, who as a teacher had mastered 'That Look', found the chair the next morning and quizzed us. We came up with some cock and bull story but her look said it all, the wise woman knew. Luckily for us they were very liberal and soon became my second parents and have seen me in many compromising situations since.

Millennium New Years Eve is just one horrific example that springs to mind. They took Thom, Jo Parsons and me to a barn party with free booze. We obviously weren't old enough to drink but had somehow managed to get a bottle of Bacardi and drunk that with orange juice (don't ask) before we had even arrived at the party. I was so looking forward to my first New Years Eve away from home, and Thom had told me they had balloons on the ceiling that were going to be released on the stroke of midnight. It was all set to be a great night. I decided in my infinite wisdom that I wanted a cocktail of every spirit that was on offer, so Thom duly obliged and looked very professional shaking it into a pint glass, which I think, if memory serves me right, only had about 2cm of cola to top it up. I downed it, and well, the rest is history. I can only recall this story thanks to photos and eyewitness testimonies. I was so smashed that I demanded all the younger kids we knew made a line from the buffet table and pass down bread and water in huge quantities to my place on the floor by the snooker table. There were ten of them passing these supplies to me like firefighters passing buckets of water to a blazing house. The plan worked a bit. I could now stand. But not for long, for my finale I crawled out from under the snooker table and landed face down into a strangers lap, and as I couldn't feel my hands or arms I was nuzzling her crotch to push my head up.

It looked VERY dodgy so I am told, and she screamed for help as Thom and Jo watched on in hysterics, laughing at me getting fresh with that poor stranger. Apparently they both had a great time, and got to see the balloons and fireworks. I came round the next morning and reached for the orange juice carton, downed it, then had the horrible realization we had mixed the Bacardi inside the orange juice carton before leaving for the party!! I have never touched Bacardi since.

Breakfast was awful; I opened the kitchen door to see no less than fifteen grown adults from the night before sitting smugly around the table. They all took it in turns to fill me in. The only thing that got me through was Nigel's (Thom's Dad) legendary scrambled egg. It was too late, I had made a name for myself, but dear Nigel and Sandra were so good to me considering this and many of our other antics. A later incident helped me live up to my newfound reputation.

The Rees family and their large group of friends and children all went to Butlins for a birthday and I was invited along, as was the norm. We all stayed on the campus and the adults had a few chalets, and the kids another. We went out the first night, got very drunk and if you have ever been to the Bognor Regis Butlins, you will know that the chalets are set out in a maze with weird names to supposedly help you locate your temporary abode. I presumed I would be going back with Thom and co, so when I found myself walking up and down Octopus Lane with not a hope in hell of finding my bed, I was delighted to stumble across a familiar looking building.

I walked up and with no key slumped myself in the hallway next to where I thought my chalet was. I was woken, not by Thom, but by a middle-aged couple and asked if I needed a room. I must have said yes. I woke up with no real memory of the night before. I looked around me and saw the couple with barely any clothes on and presumed I had been part of some gang-bang or something!! I ran out, called Thom on his mobile and found my way back to our chalet. We got changed, swapped stories then went to breakfast at the adults chalet. I told the assembled adults about my night and then, a knock at the door revealed the good Samaritan couple. "WTF" I thought, (CRINGE). Turns out they were part of our group all along, they had arrived later that evening and were on a different table to us. I just hadn't noticed them during the night out!! Oh the shame.

So even though we were poor, I still had a great childhood with friends like Thom and a loving caring Mum and extended family. We wouldn't have gone on any overseas holidays had it not been for my dear Aunty and Uncle, they used to take us once a year to Majorca to a beautiful Villa owned by a friend of theirs. It wasn't just a holiday; it was a holiday from poverty. We had a well-rounded and grounded upbringing, and thanks to my Aunt, Uncle, Gran and Grandpa it was made all the more happy, secure and comfortable.

As I reached the age of eighteen, I had a powerful realisation that there must be more to life than just working, eating, and going out getting trashed. That realisation didn't and hasn't stopped me from enjoying myself but I now feel I have a deeper understanding of what is going on in the world around me. I had forgotten all the soul-stirring things that I had experienced as a young whipper-snapper, and I was blinded by the trivial pre-occupation of being an adult.

After sixth form, I had a few years of doing random jobs in my hometown, and then moved to Gran Canaria for three months with some friends for a bit of escapism. I barely worked while I was there, all thanks to my Credit Card! Even though I had a great tan, I paid the price. On my return to the UK I owed £10k on that card. At the age of nineteen I moved to London shortly after arriving back, ready to start my new job in a Government department. As the starting salary was so low and the cost of living in London so high, I was inevitably broke. And I *mean* broke. My pay didn't even come close to covering my overdraft. My solution was to go back on the last train to the Shire (as I call it) every Friday, when the barriers were open so I could nip through without paying.

I would spend the weekend with my family and stock up on food to last me until the following Friday. When I said I had no money, I literally meant it. I had negative amounts of money every month, even after being paid. The lack of money, lack of self-confidence, and the low self-esteem I felt all contributed to my growing sense of depression. I believed my life was seemingly heading nowhere down some empty corridor towards non-greatness. I was nowhere near, not even close to fulfilling the potential I **knew** I had been gifted with – as we all are. The huge changes that had taken place in as little as two years since leaving home and education all contributed to my dark feeling of helplessness and confusion. I had dreamed of living in the big city for much of my childhood, but soon realised it was not all it was cracked up to be.

I couldn't make sense of the reason I was alive on this planet, and I simply couldn't get to grips with the point of life. I didn't know who **I** was, or who the **real me** was. I am a deep thinker, and that really didn't help matters, and neither did it help that I had the time to think so negatively, running things round my head, over and over again like a broken record. As far as I was concerned, I had hit rock bottom, crying into my pillow most nights asking why! Granted I wasn't a crack-head or homeless, but in my world, in my comparative environment, I had hit rock bottom. I believe alarm bells start to ring in all of us when we're not achieving what we are sent 'here' to do – a gentle jolt to remind us of our full potential and purpose.

Ultimately, when I look back on this period in my life, I think I was looking for the answer to the most important question we all ask at some stage; **what is the purpose and meaning of life, and where do I fit in?**

Although I was surrounded by great friends and a wonderful family who were all willing to listen and offer advice, no matter what they said I knew it wouldn't help. I had to find the solution myself. I realised my problem was not with the world or people around me, it was **within** me. So I tried reasoning with myself by comparing my situation to those in Africa and other third world countries, but I still had the same issues and problems. I didn't want people knowing that I needed help as it felt like I was admitting to failure, and therefore wasn't as strong as society makes us believe we should be. Perhaps keeping a stiff upper lip is a typically British feeling that doesn't help in these moments of distress.

On one of the countless weekly trips back to my Mum's house she suggested I read one of the first spiritual books she had ever read. She slipped it in my suitcase amongst the clean clothes, potatoes, tins, cheese and other bits and pieces, and off I went like a packhorse for another week in the 'Big City'. I shrugged it off as a nice idea but couldn't see how a book was going to help me, plus I hated reading. It wasn't until about two weeks later that I re-discovered said book in a drawer under my semi-collapsed, fifteen year old bed. So that day, a day that was about to shape the rest of my life and get me back onto *the path*, I started pessimistically reading that bizarre looking book. But the more I read, the more I was drawn in, and the pessimistic view began to fall away. Since reading that first book in my studio flat in Stockwell I have read countless Spiritual or "self help books", learning more and more principles and ideas about the world we inhabit, most of which I had an innate awareness of already. All these books have one thing in common – they teach that everyone has the ability to be happy. Damn right, so we do.

New Age books are very topical in the current climate, I found I could relate to everything they talked about. The common thread that runs through most of them is everyone's ability to change for the better, to love each other in the spiritual sense, and that this can be achieved by looking within yourself for the answers.

The combination of reading these books, observing the daily interaction of people and my surrounding environment, understanding who I am, following my intuition, and most importantly looking inwardly, have all contributed to shaping me into the person I am today. If you believe what my Mum and many of her psychic friends would have you believe I am also a Lightworker. One of many beings/energy forms sent here to help mankind head towards a collective Spiritual enlightenment to end suffering on all levels. In fact, most of you reading this book now are also Lightworkers! I am not sure how far you are willing to stretch your imagination at this stage, but you can take or leave that particular idea for now!

Only now at the ripe old age of 28 do I feel I am ready to share my spiritual journey with you. Ten years in London has seen me living in various hovels, and more recently some nicer houseshares. I am now living in Clapham in a lovely houseshare with my best friend Helen and five other great people. I have a fantastic group of friends called the urban family, and they are just that. We almost wrote to the producers of The Only Way is Essex as our lives are always eventful, packed full of fun, drama and the odd upset. We all live in the 'tri-Clapham area' so are a stones' throw away from each other. I think the people we are surrounded by are a reflection of ourselves, and I am happy to say they are all lovely! I am also in a loving and fantastic relationship.

To me, London is the best of both worlds, I enjoy the anonymity of being in a large city and having a million activities to choose from, and yet Clapham offers me a village like familiarity. Like Doris at Sainsbury's; she never fails to comment on how healthy my shopping looks, the manager at my favourite restaurant greets me like an old friend, and I bump into bar staff I am friendly with (that's probably not a good thing to admit to) on the High street. I can walk to the 'Common' and the supermarket, and have a night out on my doorstep, its perfect. I brought a one bed flat recently, but could not afford to buy in Clapham so had to buy in South East London. I love Clapham so much that I rent the flat out and continue to live in my houseshare. I am just where I want to be in my life at the moment, its all fallen perfectly into place. I can assure you it has not been a straight and narrow path and things haven't landed in my lap – it wouldn't make for an interesting read if it had!

I believe certain things we experience have the ability to change our whole direction in life, and I have had five such experiences that have rocked my world and changed my thinking. The first was my move to London where my search for happiness began. Second was moving to Iraq for eight months, including a near-death experience. Third was coming out. Fourth was the death of my older sister Vicki. The fifth and most recent was a three-month solo trip to India in 2012. These life changers and everything in-between will be unravelled throughout the Lost Keys in various ways, each chapter corresponds to a lesson (or two) that can be applied to your own life. **Some are lighthearted and fun, others less so, please bear with the deeper ones. Like life, the serious shit is usually the best teacher.**

The Lost Keys are about finding *your* inner happiness and magic, so I will wrap it up there and get on with helping you unlock the doors to happiness as simply as possible, because that's exactly what this journey of self-discovery should be – simple.

Part 2

Don't Worry Be Happy – Past Experiences

♪ *You Learn, Alanis Morissette* ♪

THE MOST IMPORTANT MESSAGE I discovered from reading hundreds of New Age books is that every person on this planet wants to be happy and doesn't want to suffer. Its obvious, but I know for a fact I wanted to be happy when I moved to London, instead of being broke, suicidal, depressed and as miserable as sin.

True happiness is our fundamental right, a fundamental need, and a fundamental desire for every single person. I think it is a human right. Surely our individual quests are built around trying to find happiness in our life? Some people search for it in a house of God, others through drugs, sex or in earning bags of money. But in order to be happy, truly happy, I think it helps if we first look at the reasons why we are unhappy. When I use the word unhappy, I don't *just* mean the people who are depressed all the time, crying at night, I also include the people who feel alone, scared, unloved, unsure, unstable, and any number of emotions that fail to bring happiness. And if you have never felt sadness in any form then you have no need to read this book Mr or Mrs Dalai Lama!

The primary reason for unhappiness, and the most difficult to deal with, are issues relating to your own childhood and upbringing. Most of my friends and relatives who have been, or who are currently unhappy with their lives have underlying issues relating to their past. If you can't let go of something that hurt you emotionally in the past how can you ever expect to live in the present and move forward? Let's stop carrying all our old hurt with us each time something "negative" happens. Imagine those bad memories and emotions like a huge suitcase you are dragging behind you – if you keep on adding to the load it will eventually slow you down. **Deal** with it at the time, learn a lesson from it (there is one to be found in **all** experiences) and then you don't need to put it in that ever growing suitcase only to be told at check-in you are over the limit.

Everyone has their own way of dealing with painful issues but I imagine most people deal with them in the same way – by suppressing their painful memories so deeply into their subconscious that it ends up becoming a part of who they are. This is not a healthy way to deal with problems, and I am of the firm belief that suppressed emotions eventually manifest into physical illnesses and become the negative characteristics of our personalities.

I had huge difficulty dealing with past experiences myself. Whilst married, my Dad was extremely violent to my Mum and threatened to kill her on a number of occasions. Not empty threats either, actual intent – some say he was a touch unstable! He would constantly and unexpectedly lash out and shout at the top of his voice. When I was only 2 ½ years old and Mum was holding me in her arms in the kitchen of their farmhouse in Wiltshire, he came at her with a carving knife. She had to run upstairs with me and lock us in the bathroom while she called and waited for the police. After that experience I told everyone who came to our house that "Daddy looked really evil, his eyes were horrible and me and Mummy were really scared". They inevitably divorced and separated when I was five years old, probably for the best. After they divorced he came to visit once a week and took Laura and I out for day trips, eventually the trips became few and far between, and one day he never came back. On his last visit he told us to go and put our coats on, so we ran upstairs to get ready and came downstairs to find he had gone. We asked what we had done wrong, but Mum told us "Daddy wasn't well and it was not our fault". I guess after the last visit I must have felt rejected and hurt. Laura asked Mum about two years later "If I am a good girl Mummy, will Daddy come back to visit me?"

Even though we probably suppressed this form of rejection it was bound to play a huge part in our personalities as we grew older. As I grew up I was afraid to trust any men, and I felt intimidated and vulnerable whenever I was in the company of an older man or heard raised voices. Who could bloody blame me? On some level, our childhood experiences make us believe that our parental figures are the norm and replicated in the rest of society. I had decided to blame my reaction on my upbringing, and hoped it would go away with time. As I grew older and became more aware, I realised that if I was going to change and improve myself, then I would have to wise up and stop blaming my parents for my adult issues.

I believed the solution was to start searching inside and evaluating my behaviour. If you look at your past experiences and link these to any bad traits that you have as an adult, you will be able to see the connection. This is painfully hard, I can assure you, but worth every bit of soul searching. It is never easy to take responsibility for your own faults, but it is important so you can move forward and be happy. If you find it particularly difficult finding any bad traits, then the best way to discover your faults is to recognise what behaviour you find annoying in other people, then ask yourself if you have a tendency to behave in the same way. More often than not, what we dislike in others is a mirror of our own faults!

Once you have realised your bad traits, and learnt to let go by dealing with the underlying issues, then you can begin to correct them. Consciously knowing your faults and their origin is the only way to overcome them and improve yourself as a person. I thought to myself, "Why should I be scared of raised voices, it happened over fourteen years ago. Not everyone who shouts is going to harm my Mum, my family, or me. It wasn't my fault my Dad was a tad loopy." Once I began to really think about this logically, and after many evenings spent quietly evaluating the simplicity of the situation – it worked, I had removed the stupid drama that was controlling my whole life and personality. I also realised there was a valuable lesson to be learnt from this whole life shaping experience – imagine if my parents had not divorced, where would I be now? The all-female household I was raised in would never have existed, my Mum would probably never have deepened her spiritual beliefs, and I in turn would not have been so lucky to learn the benefits of New Age thinking. I would have also been subjected to witnessing violence and aggression for eighteen years of my life! It happened for a reason, and I can now fully accept that.

I think most past experiences that negatively affect our lives are a result of parental actions or beliefs inflicted on us during childhood – consciously or not. The way to look at this is we are all human and we all make mistakes. We've all made countless mistakes, and although we sometimes perceive our parents as being faultless, we must remember that they too are human and have not been trained to be parents. There is no right way to bring up a child. Your parents guide you according to how they think you should be brought up, more often than not in a similar manner to the way they were raised. If they made mistakes with your upbringing, forgive them. You can blame your parents all you like but at the end of the day it's up to you to progress and correct any mistakes they have made. If left unchecked, the destructive aspects can filter down the generations, and the drama will affect every generation until someone learns to deal with it and breaks the cycle. Alternatively, you can carry on blaming your parents! I know which path I chose, and I know which path solved my problem.

Something my Mum recently asked me was "Did you feel rejected when Rob (my Dad) stopped visiting you so suddenly?" And I suppose most people in my situation would have said, "Yes", but, on reflection, I had already worked on these feelings when I was much younger. I was, and still am quite introvert, I ask myself questions all the time and enjoy my own company a great deal.

When I was about thirteen and all the other kids had their Dads supporting them at sports days; cheering them on, giving pep talks, I began to ask myself why my Dad never visited little old me anymore. I remember it well. We were all sitting in a line preparing to do the rather pointless British game of running while keeping an egg on a spoon, when I saw my friend's Dad on the sidelines taking a picture of my friend and giving him the thumbs up sign. After asking myself the question, I came to the conclusion that it must have hurt him too much to keep coming and going and leaving us behind each time. So by this self-evaluation (Mum later confirmed this was actually the case!) I learnt to deal with his absence in a positive way, rather than beat myself up about it, and blame myself for what were ultimately his issues.

Find a way of dealing with the issues that have affected you. Take some time out to think about what has affected you in a negative way to shape you into the person you are today. This doesn't just stop at childhood issues, it can also include influences that affect us later in life such as the death of a loved one, or failed relationships, abortion, abuse even.

Why not take just one hour on a lazy Sunday afternoon to lock yourself in your bedroom, or to take a bath and think about these issues. Write them down if it helps, speak them aloud – whatever it takes to bring them to the surface. Book a time slot in your diary just for you.

This will be the single biggest step you will ever take to improve yourself, your happiness and your spirituality. Who can't afford to do that? I call it **emotional purging.**

I had a 'purge' recently while on my soul-searching trip in India. It had been a while since I had done one and it's amazing what came up. I just lay there, staring at the ceiling; no music, no TV, no phone, and I just let my mind be. I let my mind think what it wanted, and let things come up. Some people popped into my head so I followed the thought.

I cried lots, I cried about things I didn't even know had affected me, I cried for people I hadn't thought about or seen for years. It all needed to come up and out. Then I made a vow to do something about the things I could change. I am going to see my Gran more often before it is too late, and I am going to contact a foster Brother who has gone off the rails. I also realised I felt guilty about hurting an ex by ending a relationship, and that was from five years previously.

After these sessions of looking back on life, crying, and letting go, I felt much lighter and at ease. It really helps. Just find the time and let it come up to the surface, don't force it, just let it be.

Ask yourself; do you have difficulty trusting people? Are you scared of being hurt in relationships? Do you feel as though people are attacking you verbally? Do you speak too much to cover up silences? Do you get scared when you hear raised voices? Do you sleep around to feel loved? Do you feel lonely all the time? Do you rock the boat and start arguments unnecessarily? Are you aggressive, or easily frustrated? Do you feel a need to show off your intelligence? Do you like to control everything? Are you overly competitive? Do you complain for sympathy? Do you seek attention all the time? Do you like to create drama regardless of the consequences? Do you get pleasure from putting people down? Do you secretly like being ill or injured?

So many issues that affect us in adulthood are a direct result of the negativity we experience during childhood and throughout our lifetime. Bring your issues to the surface and deal with them. It might be a little painful at first, but you **need** to do it. You **have** to do it for yourself. Learn from the negatives in life – that's why they crop up so you can learn the valuable lessons first hand. **That is one of the biggest secrets of the universe!** These things occur for the sole reason of education – they are to be learnt from. They won't go away until you learn a positive lesson from them. On a deeper Spiritual level we need these 'negative' experiences for our own development. Everyone will experience the lows and negatives of life, some more than others, some less than others, but we all come across them. Without the lows we cannot experience, compare and enjoy the highs. So use this secret to your advantage and see the hidden meaning in what is happening to you. Ask yourself "why" more often, and discover the reasons, often a negative situation has a positive twist. It will quickly lead you to happiness and away from misery, making you a more rounded individual. Soon you'll be travelling with only small hand luggage instead of that oversized baggage you've been dragging around for far too long.

Find time in your diary next Sunday and start evaluating YOU. It will be the beginning of a life-changing chapter in your life, the first of a very exciting book.

2

More To Life Than Working 9-5 – Spirituality

♪ *Bring Me To Life, Evanescence* ♪

Since leaving school and starting work I always believed there had to be something more than a 9-5 existence, some greater purpose for our lives than waking up and working eight hours a day in some dead-end job. It turns out there is, and its called Spirituality. What is spirituality I hear you cry? Well, being spiritual does not mean you need to worship a God or follow a religion. Spirituality is a word that I will be using quite broadly throughout this book so here is my interpretation of Spirituality – empathy, balance, harmony, inner and outer peace, unconditional love, happiness, self-evaluation, compassion, contemplation, confidence, change, truth, self improvement, stability, nature, respect and, of course, mind power. These qualities all make up the word spirituality but, ultimately, I see spirituality as **a new way of looking at the world and at the things that happen to you. It's a new mindset for a new age in humanity.**

Once we have dealt with our past experiences the next step is to decide what we want from life. This may sound an obvious statement, so hold your horses before shouting "money"… I don't mean the usual; good job, money, nice car and a couple of holidays a year. All these things are materialistic. What happens when you get that house, or get that shiny new car? What next? Material objects and possessions will bring a feeling of happiness for a limited period. Once you have all the material things you want, then you live with the constant fear that the money will run out or be taken away from you. Constantly wanting more will not make you happy.

Take, for example, the number of celebrities with enough wealth to last several lifetimes. Most of them keep searching for more wealth, more fun times, more drugs, more alcohol, more publicity, more highs, and they end up on a path of self-destruction, taking it to extremes and wrecking their careers or even committing suicide. Britney Spears is just one example. As I am writing this she has just checked out of rehab and I am pretty sure that if she doesn't decide what is important to her, then it won't be the last time she checks-in and out again.

Robbie Williams who was constantly in and out of rehab is another fitting example. It appears that even with all his wealth (the last I heard he had signed a record deal for £80 million) he is still not content, and searching for more (written in 2007). Until he discovers some sort of belief system, or maybe love, I don't think he will ever find what he is looking for. On the flip side of this, Madonna who has been around for a few generations and re-invented herself more times than most, seems to be comfortable with the wealth she has accumulated during her career. It just so happens she found an ancient form of religion (Kabala) and other new age practices such as Yoga. Madonna, who is one of the wealthiest celebrities, found a non-materialistic purpose. She is compassionate and charitable, and it just so happens she is happy and content. I hope this goes someway to explaining the importance of trying to find a non-materialistic belief system.

There are no right or wrong Philosophies, Religions, or New Age belief systems, only those that work best for the individual. Wars have started because some people have believed the very opposite to that last sentence.

We will each find the right belief system for us, at the right time. Personally I don't believe in Christianity, or any of the Western religious views. Although contentious, I think the whole Christianity belief system is founded on lies and twisted truths. I am sure there was a man called Jesus Christ but I believe he was simply a man of great compassion, love, strength of mind, and a very centred spiritual individual (spiritual in the sense of understanding his inner power), who was turned into a figure of religious worship for millions of followers throughout the ages. He was attractive to the people who had lost touch with their innate understanding of the world. Many theorists believe that Christianity stopped civil wars and unrest in the ancient civilisations and created a faith for the public to follow. It gave them something to believe in, rules to follow, and a higher power to answer to. Fear has a habit of controlling the masses. There are also theories that the creation of Christianity gave power to the churches and the men that run them. The select few who edited and created the scriptures, held in their hands the power to control and influence millions of people whilst at the same time earning money from their newly created 'religion'. What could be a more perfect business venture for the greedy men of those times? Have the people live in fear so they will obey the church's doctrine, and pay into its' coffers.

Christians, Muslims and other religious groups have all murdered millions in the name of their religion. Some of these crusades/ holy wars had the sole intention of stamping out uprisings, or people that held a slightly different viewpoint from their own. How can a religion that doesn't tolerate individual choice or the right to live be religious or good?

If I believed in a God (which I don't), I would think it was his choice, and his alone to kill the humans he created. People were burnt alive at the stake, blinded, dragged behind horses, tortured, and children and woman brutally massacred on instructions from the ordained members of those so called religions. I find that stomach churning and if such a God exists, I do not believe for one second he would advocate that brutality in his name. This is yet another reason on my long list as to why I personally do not subscribe to these particular religions.

From a New Age perspective I believe in the total power of the mind and its ability to transform everything in my world. I also believe in the healing power of crystals, light and sound, psychic abilities, synchronicity, Karma, Re-incarnation, Astrology, Numerology, Dowsing, Meditation, Metaphysics, and the importance of dreams. To be honest I don't know a great deal about all religions, but I mostly associate with Buddhism. However, I can clearly see the underlying message in all religions. They are trying to get the same message across in their own way. One of the key re-occurring messages is that we should all **love and respect each other**, regardless of race, sex, and religious beliefs. This is a great message as far as I am concerned, and yet this same message seems to have been twisted, distorted and not actually followed. How ironic to think we have been fighting holy wars all the way back to the year 0000 for this very reason.

Christianity tells us to love thy neighbour, Buddhism tells us to have compassion for all living things, Islam emphasises the importance of the family unit and to treat others well, and Judaism tells us to love our neighbours as ourselves. If only all religions could agree on just one piece of common ideology – every single living creature's desire to be happy and not to suffer. We could then be united in that one belief, despite following different paths in order to reach it.

Respect comes from understanding that we are all different, we are born into different situations and circumstances, and therefore all have a right to follow different paths to reach a common goal. So there are no right or wrong paths, and by the same token, there are no right or wrong religions.

I don't confess to be a true Buddhist but I follow my own system. I meditate 2-3 times a week and don't kill any animals whatsoever (including the smaller things in life like flies and spiders). I became a vegetarian in October 2006 (and will explain this in a later Lost Key), I have compassion and empathy for everyone that crosses my path, and I strongly believe in Karma – what you give out you get back. I believe that every thought we have, good or bad, will manifest itself one way or another in the physical world, and I appreciate the beauty on this planet, from an ant to a sunset over the Himalayas. Some of the *original strands* of Buddhism make **so** much sense to me. Their religion is Godless – they have never worshipped an idol of any description, they simply practice the laws of the middle way (a balanced outlook that leads to a state of peace). Compared to all other religions that now seem to lack substance, believable teachings and meaningful doctrines, Buddhism really strikes a chord with me. I see it more as a philosophy and way of life than a religion. It is simply a different way to view the world by mastering the mind – the source of all unhappiness. The Dali Lama is a shining example of the peaceful way of Buddhism.

I was lucky enough to meet the Dali Lama at St Paul's

Cathedral in London. I met him in the crypts of St Paul's where candles and chanting filled the catacombs and created a surreal atmosphere.

He had an incredibly peaceful and happy presence. He shook my hand and in that moment I felt a wave of calmness wash through my body and mind. It was a magical experience, and one I won't forget in a hurry.

On another work visit, to Jerusalem, I had the opportunity to visit the Holy quarters where I spent two hours walking around the ancient cobbled, walled city. Through the winding alleys and market stalls that resembled something out of Arabian Nights, I reached an open courtyard swarming with people from all walks of life. I entered a church that was supposedly built on top of the Tomb of Christ. There were hundreds of people queuing to kiss various artefacts and areas within the church, and one memory stands out to this day. I saw a frail old lady surrounded by her family, she kissed a stone that seemed to be some kind of large altar stone and then suddenly, spontaneously, burst into tears, started weeping, shaking, and was absolutely inconsolable. It made me think that if someone places such strong emotions and such faith in a religion, how can it be wrong? If their belief brings happiness and a sense of peace and security *without* harming others then who am I to criticise their belief system? As I walked around the church and observed the variety of people that had probably intended to make this pilgrimage for decades, I asked myself why they all put so much faith in prayer. But I realised this wasn't a question I should be asking. The question I should have been asking is why prayer works for people?

I found my time in Jerusalem bizarrely homely and very surreal – as if I had been there before or was picking up on a positive energy. As I sat on a wall watching the people, I came to the conclusion that prayer was a method of putting faith in something else in order to provide answers or intervention. I feel that some prayers work because so much thought and such strong belief is placed upon them that they manifest in the physical world and become reality. I believe in the total power of the mind, and I personally don't see any need to put faith in a God who we cannot see and does not exist (in my view). We should live according to our own moral compass, and realise there is no one person looking down and judging us; that is something we should do ourselves. **We all have the power of a God-like figure *within* us, without the need to worship an all powerful, omnipresent deity.**

We perceive what we want to, and no one else can see into our individual and personal universes. We each have the power to make choices, decisions, and to take control of our life and destiny. We are each a "God" capable of achieving anything. Our minds, our outlook, our natural ability to interpret our surroundings are all more than capable of coping with what life throws at us – and this is what I believe "God" is. But if prayer works, or provides a system of faith and belief, then fair enough, go ahead and pray. It forces the mind to focus intently on a desired outcome with absolute faith – a certain way of achieving what you want. I can't deny that.

Our mind is something we can take absolute responsibility for, and complete control over, and it is something more tangible than any form of God. It takes a great amount of trust and **self-belief** to know you have complete control over everything in your life, without the need to look upward for answers or direction. It gives you responsibility that was once entrusted to the heavens. **Everything that happens to you is created by you, by your thoughts, and by you alone.** If you can accept that, and live with that thought in the back of your mind every moment, I think you have grasped what Gurus and Enlightened beings have searched for and found, for as long as time immemorial. Most people find this a scary thought as it literally replaces God and transfers all the power and responsibility to the individual. This is hard to accept but will enhance your Spirituality if you are able to do so. Even the bible quotes Jesus as saying "that we can do what he does" and that "we are made in his image".

While I think of it, I just want to say a few things about sins in religious teachings. As I have said, I personally don't believe in any of the monotheistic religions (Christianity, Judaism, or Islam). I think they were written by people of power and influence many years ago in order to gain some control over the public within their geographical location. They also tried to make sense of the universe and of the simple rising and setting of the sun. I think what they called "sins" were basically what we would call "laws" nowadays. Laws change with the times and are replaced, edited, and added to. However, religious texts need to remain unchanged to show integrity as sacred historical writings or the whole religion falls into disrepute.

The Church cannot re-write their sins as governments re-write their laws, even though their followers' attitudes, environment and lifestyles have changed so dramatically through the centuries. Imagine if our government had not changed laws since they were first invented! We would live in a world of chaos. There would be no laws covering traffic, protected species, taxes, or child internet pornography… I could go on and on, but as you can see, we have changed and evolved as a species, and so have the laws we abide by.

If the afore-mentioned religions, with their strict and numerous sins, ever tried to update their "laws", their very foundations would crack. Signs of this are already showing all over the world – lack of attendance at houses of worship, religious wars, a sense of unrest, and generally a lack of interest in the teachings. We as humans have evolved, and the various religious teachings that once supported and complemented society have not evolved because, in my view, they were not truthful in the first place. They no longer fit our modern world anymore, so how can they be from God, if they don't make sense in the present moment?

That is why so many people have the feeling that something is missing from their lives, are feeling lonely or incomplete, uncertain or anxious. "Traditional" religions simply don't answer our questions, or at least parts of them don't, which begs the question that if religious teachings are Godly, Spiritual, and truthful, then should they not fit every stage of human evolution?

Buddhism appears to be one religion capable of maintaining integrity throughout human evolution.

Every guiding principle I have come across still manages to apply to the present day, just as it did 2500 odd years ago. That says so much to me. We need something to believe in, and I don't think the majority of the religions cut the mustard anymore!

Here is a short, but very important snippet into the evolution of human existence – we hunted and ate to stay alive, then moved forward a few thousand years where we preoccupied ourselves with strict religious teachings. We then went through the scientific age – attempting to rationalise and categorise the mysteries of the universe and our surroundings with science, and finally and most recently we adopted an economic attitude (earning money to "enjoy" ourselves and our scientific advances). None of which have achieved the ultimate quest in our life – to be happy and content individuals. We are now entering a period of evolution where the human race is finally ready to discover the true answers. **This is called the New Age, and it's about finding the "God" within each of us.**

We all need a belief system in our life, if only to act as a balance to our working days, a belief in the New Age, a Philosophy, or a real religion. As humans we are naturally very inquisitive, and one of the most difficult questions we ask at some point is – "**what is the purpose of life?**" By having contemplated what, who, and why you are here, you can go some way to answering this. I am sure you will agree it is not to work 9-5, five times a week – to be repeated for more or less fifty odd years of our lifetime? Can this **really** be why we are here, why we exist, why we think the thoughts we are capable of thinking?

Some people of my Mum's generation believed that their purpose was to simply find love, marry, have kids, work to provide for their families, be as successful as possible and then die.

They reach the age of retirement, look back and ask themselves why they wasted the best years of their life on this planet. I for one do not want to reach such a shitty realisation. Fast forward thirty years and I refuse to look back and think, "I wish I had done that, or experienced this". This thought makes me want to live my life to the full, achieve my dreams, devouring all of the mysteries and opportunities life has to offer me, and drink the cup of life bone-dry. Who knows when we will reach our sell-by dates?!

I am pretty sure that you have thought at one point or another "there seems to be something missing in my life and I can't work out what that is", or perhaps you suffer from anxiety, a feeling of emptiness, or a feeling of loneliness. Having a more profound and aware belief system will help you deal with those very issues. You can have all the money in the world or keep as busy as possible, but there will always be that nagging feeling in the back of your mind or in your heart that something is missing, until you find 'it' outside the "material" you. You just need to see the world in a different way. It's like putting on a pair of 3D glasses.

This can be found when you spend time on your Spiritual development, by looking inward and finding a belief system that is right for you. Nine times out of ten it will just involve opening your mind and changing your mindset. It's about your higher purpose on this planet, about getting in touch with your reason for living.

Our intuition – often called coincidences – those moments of déjà vu, sensing bad or good vibes from people, thinking about a person and then hearing from or bumping into them, moments of synchronicity that answer questions or put you on a desired path – they all stem from what some people call the Soul or Spirit. It's the thing above the mind, something that hasn't been proved by our scientists but that we can all relate to, and have experienced in some shape or form.

Just think of all those unexplainable moments in life we shrug off and try to rationalise. Simple things like dreams – they don't just happen because it is part of the sleeping process. They are messages from something higher than us, higher than the unconscious, they are messages that need to be deciphered and worked on, listened to and acted upon. I like to call that higher something the Spirit, as 'Soul' sounds too religious for my liking (I hope I am not beginning to sound like an anti-religious devil worshiper as I continue to write this!) ... Anyway, it's that higher thing we need to get back in touch with, that we have rationalised and ignored for too long. I will go into more simplified detail about the Spirit in The Lost Key on Karma.

Find the belief system that is right for you and you will find happiness, and a state of contentment will not be far behind. You are a "God" and have the capability to do anything. Re-awaken the messages your Spirit wants you to remember and you will find your purpose for living. Try and remember you are so much more than a human machine working 9-5, there is more to your existence on this planet, and the point of life is to find out what that is. Follow what feels right in your heart, not what your mind tells you!

3

Kick Me When I am Down – Setbacks & Expectations

♪ Bring It All Back – Club Seven ♪

Trust me when I say I know what it feels like to experience setbacks in life – ones that have the ability to bring you down, make you unhappy, and where you feel as if you are constantly swimming against the current. We will all experience any number of setbacks, it's simply part of life. I think I have had more than my fair share, I actually got to the stage where I was sure 'something' out there was deliberately trying to make things difficult for me, a dark force sabotaging my life to make everything difficult. I thought I was cursed with bad luck and everything felt like a constant uphill bloody struggle. As crazy as it sounds I began to think I was on a reality show with actors and actresses all around me making my life hell for good entertainment!

Nothing went my way – from simple things like waking up late and missing my pre-paid £1 Megabus back to my Mum's house in the countryside to get my weekly rations of food, to not getting jobs I had set my heart on. I crashed my Mum's car into a neighbour's wall when I was sixteen and under the influence of gallons of White Lightning and had to pay off the cost of the wall and the car over three years. Let's just say my Mum's reaction was not exactly spiritual on that occasion! After living in Gran Canaria and racking up £10k of debt I was trying to think of imaginative ways to pay it off, so I once flew back there on a Friday night, stayed with my good friend Danni, brought 20,000 cigarettes and flew back via Madrid on the Sunday with the intention of selling them for a massive mark up which would have paid for my flights, the fags, and a significant amount of my debt.

On arrival in Heathrow I walked through the "nothing to declare" green channel as bold as brass and thought "at last, something is going my way." Not so, lurking round the corner of that corridor was an army of customs officers who made a beeline straight for me. They put my huge suitcase on one of the tables in full view of all the other people sheepishly making their way through the corridor. They asked me where I had come from, "Madrid" I replied, as it would have been legal to bring back 20,000 fags from there, rather than Gran Canaria. They opened my suitcase, lifted up the one towel and minimal clothing I had packed, then like a waterfall, 1000 individual packets cascaded onto the floor. I went bright red and said they were for personal use but they pointed out that a security sticker on my suitcase indicated that I had flown in from Gran Canaria, and I was only allowed 200. They stuffed a black bin bag full with the surplus fags and I was given a caution and sent on my way. That one label had been my downfall, if I had peeled it off I would have been fine, but it pushed me even more into the red. Needless to say I didn't risk it again.

Those are just a few of many examples I could give. We have all been there with these types of experiences, and become angry, upset, or downhearted. But now I am more aware of the way the world works and my purpose for being here, I can see all setbacks happen for a reason. **Everything that ever happens to you happens for a reason**. If you can remember that when you experience life's setbacks, you will begin to see the silver linings, and realise how true that statement actually is. If you can't see the reason now for the incident, if you reflect on it afterwards you will find one – I guarantee it. On the very few occasions when I really couldn't find a reason, I put it down to a simple lesson in patience. The lessons will guide you towards your true path in life, and they force you to see the fantastic mysteries around each corner, and behind each setback. Have a little faith (I wish there was a less religious word I could use here) that there is a good reason behind a seemingly negative action, and it will eventually show itself. I promise that with all my heart, and everything I own.

If you take for example the time I was living at home with my Mum shortly after leaving school. I had just finished my AS levels and was working full time in Littlewoods Index (a catalogue order shop). I had no idea what kind of career I wanted and found myself in a state of limbo. Every night I was on the Internet looking for jobs I thought might be interesting. Eventually, after talking to Katy Morgan who was a good friend of mine at the time, I decided to become an Events Organiser. The job description fitted me like a glove so I sat down and wrote a CV, sending it to no less than fifty companies in London. Every single one of those companies wrote back and said I needed more experience or they had no vacancies. I kept all of the rejection letters as an incentive to motivate myself, and so with much encouragement from my good old Mum I decided to get that experience they were all asking for. I needed at least two years office experience with some experience of organising events so I hunted for office jobs in London and Milton Keynes.

Jane Effemey (a friend of my Mum's) told me about a vacancy at her work and arranged for an interview. I went to the interview and thought it went incredibly well, I was quite confident I had snapped up the job, but alas, a week later I was told that I wasn't suitable for the job. I was gutted that I had put in so much effort and received nothing in return. Back to square one again. A month went by, and as I was in a stable job and had no more motivation I just plodded along and didn't bother looking for any more office jobs. I could have quite easily stayed at Littlewoods Index for the rest of my life and slowly worked my way up, but in the back of my mind

I still had the desire for a better job, more suited to my interests and capabilities. Also I didn't see why I should just settle for the easy option (this thought has become a great motivational tool in all areas of my life).

Then one Sunday afternoon I saw an article in a paper recruiting office staff in a Government department in London called the Foreign Office. London being the place I had dreamed of living for most of my life, the bright lights were finally calling! I applied, and was sent a questionnaire the size of a small book. My application was successful, so a series of independent tests followed. I found the first test really difficult so I naturally thought I had fluffed it. To my surprise after six months of waiting I was told I had passed the test, and security checks. I was then asked to attend an interview. I blagged a few of the questions and thought I had failed at the last hurdle, but I kept my cool throughout and two weeks later was offered the job (out of a thousand candidates!) and signed the Official Secrets Act.

I was in that job for ten years and was very lucky. What was initially a job to gain office experience turned out to be an amazing opportunity. I travelled the world, stayed in some amazing places, met fantastic people, including a number of world leaders and royalty, and have been privy to information that only the Prime Minister and a small number of other people have seen, including me, so I feel very privileged. Of course I can never tell anyone else for as long as I live, but it's nice to know these things none the less! I also discovered an Event Organising section within this Department and held a job with them for just over a year, realising that it wasn't for me after all! This is one example that things really do happen for a reason. I <u>know</u> that I didn't get all those other Event Organising jobs because I was destined for a better one – the one I have at the moment. Maybe the reason I didn't get 20,000 fags through customs was because it would have put me on a path of crime.

The key is to see the hidden meaning behind anything that you consider a setback. Look deep, and think outside the box and you will begin to see meaning in everything that happens to you, be it good or bad. With this outlook you can be sure that nothing will get you down and unsettle your internal balance. This realisation is a magical feeling. If you choose to look at the world as hell and see nothing but misery, trouble, and setbacks then that's how it will be. **YOU CAN DECIDE** how you perceive the world around you, and that's what makes us humans so special, we all perceive things differently from each other. There is no right or wrong way to perceive the world and experiences we encounter, but there are particular perceptions that have the ability to influence your life in a more positive way than others. That said, don't kid yourselves or become blind either; there are people in mental institutions with very warped perceptions of this world that aren't necessarily wrong, but do more harm than good.

Things will happen to you in every moment of your life; even if you locked yourself away in solitary confinement you would still experience feelings and emotions that can be learnt from, so wherever you are, whatever you are doing, make sure you learn from all experiences. Seeing the lessons will become easier with time, but the key thing to remember is our idea of setbacks 'setting us back' are all wrong, **they are in fact driving us forward.** They teach us the lessons first hand that we wouldn't otherwise experience. We really need to experience them.

Just when I was beginning to think that nothing bad ever happens to me, I was sent another lesson in the form of a 'setback'! I brought my first flat in 2012 and although people warned me that the property market was a nightmare, I didn't believe them, I thought it should be an easy process. It wasn't. After receiving the keys three weeks later than planned because of the previous owners debts, I had a week to get it ready, get my tenant moved in, and then leave the next day for my three-month soul searching trip to India. The flat only needed a lick of paint and a bit of gardening, or so I thought. On day one of that hellish week I discovered the toilet and taps didn't work so I called a plumber, he fixed them for a ridiculous fee, and it seemed all was back on track. It was a sunny and perfectly still June day, and as I was staring into the garden thinking "I should prune that tree", said tree cracked and fell in a giant slow motion arc, straight onto the neighbour's fence. The plumber and neighbour both jumped out of their skin and asked what I had done. I replied, "nothing, it just fell by itself".

I had a sinking feeling that this could be the start of something horrible! Day four arrived and I returned to find a huge leak in the kitchen ceiling from the bathroom above, and the ceiling had partially collapsed. The central heating didn't work either so I called a plumber again (they are very expensive if you haven't had the privilege!). Apparently the entire system was unsafe and needed new pipes throughout. I now had two days to fix a ceiling, fix a leak, get a new boiler, new pipes and sort the garden. After the various handymen had surveyed the damage and left, I sat on the floor, broke down, and asked myself why this was all happening. My flight was already booked and I had spent all my money on buying the sodding flat, so every expense was a new blow to the head. On top of all that I just couldn't get the labourers to come at such short notice.

I spoke to my Mum and brother Simon (a Site Manager) too many times to count, and in the end realised there was no point fighting it, I just had to get on with it, call hundreds of people, borrow the extra dosh and just pay whatever they wanted.

The next day I had two plasterers, four plumbers in the flat, plus the Extreme Makeover Team comprising my little sis Laura, her boyfriend Steve, best mate Helen, and my boyfriend Jolyon. I had to push the move-in date back by two days, and change my flight for an extra £300, we finished with one hour to spare, and the paint still drying.

The next day I ran round central London and brought all my travelling clothes on credit, went straight to the airport, and while sitting drinking a glass of well-deserved champagne I contemplated what the hidden lesson could be. I realised it was better for all that stuff to happen before the tenant moved in, instead of when I was cooped-up in some Ashram in the Himalayas and was unable to do much about it. Who knows, the original flight I had booked might have crashed, or my connecting bus that would take me up the mountains may have come off the road. Also, when I left Heathrow Terminal 3 I was completely exhausted, stressed, un-centred and basically a shell of a man – and it was in this state that I entered India. On reflection I was more open to the lessons I learned in this broken down state than I would have been if that week from hell hadn't happened. At the time I couldn't see why it was happening to me and I felt kicked in the face by the Universe, but I was certain there was a reason for it. Now I am grateful that it all happened at just the right time, and it helped me grow even more as a person.

One vital piece of advice for anyone experiencing a setback is sometimes it is **just better to accept it**. It is ten times easier if you can accept what is thrown at you rather than fight it. We will always be given situations or experiences to learn from when we need the lessons. Someone wisely said "we are never given more than we can handle" and I believe that. A number of 'setbacks' could happen to you in one month, or be spaced out over a decade, who knows. You'll get these opportunities when you need them, trust in that. It is the school of life, educating us along the way through hardship, pain and sorrow. We do also learn through the good experiences but less so – typical really! Just know that they will help you in the long run, find the hidden meaning and you will be fine.

Expectations also have a similar way of shaping our futures. I know I have had a spirituality privileged upbringing with a fantastic Mum, and she will no doubt feature many times throughout The Lost Keys. She has never had any expectations of me, and only asked me to, "try your best darling, because that's all any of us can ever do". Which makes perfect sense – if you have tried your best at achieving something, then if you don't succeed at least you know you tried 100% and it simply wasn't meant to be.

It is better to give your all than to have doubt that it was through your own laziness you failed. This method of thinking also stopped me worrying about events before they occurred. If you really have done all you can, then you should have nothing to worry about. And even if you haven't done all you can do, there comes a point where you have no further influence over the outcome, so there is no point in worrying anyway – it will achieve absolutely sod all. After that moment in time, the decision is out of your hands and with someone else; worrying will solve nada.

While at the Foreign Office, I had to complete a written bidding form for a new job within the office. I put so much time and effort to make it appeal to the prospective department that I must have re-drafted it about fifteen times. Once I had sent it to HR I felt happy that I had done my best, and if I didn't get the job then I was destined for something else. I sat back and didn't think about the result until they contacted me and told me, on that occasion, I was successful. If I had worried about the result I would have become stressed and run hundreds of "what if" scenarios through my head – "What if I had done it that way, or this way, or not put that in, or told them that instead". I am sure you have had many 'what if' scenarios run through your head in the past. Playing the 'what if' game with yourself is such a complete waste of precious time. Who cares? What is done is done, get over it! Jolyon once said to me "We will celebrate if you get the job, and celebrate if you don't get the job – either way, it will be the right decision". These wise words contain an *enormous* amount of truth.

I was lucky not to have been put under any pressure, but I have noticed that some of my friends were put under, or are still under a lot of pressure to perform well, either from parents or other people in their lives, and some obviously crack the whip on themselves too much. Parents don't necessarily have to verbally put their kids under pressure as I discovered when talking to a friend of the family a few years back. If a parental figure is very successful materially, their kids can feel that they need to compete and prove themselves as equals. Any type of pressure, including self-imposed, puts a huge strain on a person both mentally and spiritually.

To any parents reading this, ask yourself if you are putting too much pressure on your kids? It is natural for any parent to want their children to do well, but I don't think it's fair to put such huge weight on the shoulders of young people, because it's hard enough growing up in this modern fast-paced world without having the additional pressure from those closest to you.

If you feel under pressure from parents, try and take a step back and always remember that it is **your** life, you were given the opportunity to do **<u>anything</u>** with it. No one else should dictate how you should live it. It is important to realise that you won't find happiness from making other people happy, unless it's also what you truly want from life. So start pleasing yourself.

The hardest thing to do is take responsibility for your own choices, but that is exactly what you must do in order to break free from any pressures that are imposed on you. Decide what is important to you, and take on the responsibilities that are associated with those choices. In order to deal with any pressure from parents don't get angry with them, you should try and work out why they are expecting so much from you. I think it could be for one of two reasons:

- Firstly it could be because they simply love you and only want to see you do well but are perhaps going about it the wrong way. They get caught up with wanting the best for you and only see the end goal and not how it is affecting you at the present moment. I suppose there would be an element of "it's for the greater good" in their thinking. Their justification for pushing you so hard could be a little bit of pressure now pays off in the long term.

- Secondly, it could be because they are trying to live their life through you. Often when parents don't realise their dreams and feel they are too old, or have too many restrictions, they tend to push those dreams onto their children, and with this comes the pressure to succeed where they failed.

If you think either points above are true then the best solution would be to approach them diplomatically and lay it on the table and talk things over. I find that when people are confronted with their faults and issues they make an effort to change them for the better. Sometimes it's only when a loved-one points out our failings that we realise we have them. Just put it tactfully, calmly and without making them feel in anyway threatened or bullied, and they will understand where you are coming from, at the same time realising their mistakes. "Do as you would be done unto" – or whatever that religious quote reads!

This method will also work with any situation where you need to confront people about their actions towards you – its all in the approach and delivery! For example, I wouldn't take on board anything someone said to me if they were shouting, because I would instantly presume they were out of control. By the same token I wouldn't expect anyone to listen to me if I was shouting, or if I came across in an aggressive manner.

If you feel as though you are under pressure to do well in life because your parents have done so, then it is worth talking this through with them. Say how you feel and I am sure they will put you right and make you realise that these feelings are unjustified. "You" are not "your parents", and you have no need to compete with them. If this pressure stems from something they have never actually said to you, then it must be something you have said to yourself. Ask yourself why you feel that way? Remember that initial feeling or moment in time when you decided that you needed to put so much pressure on yourself to 'succeed'. Once you find that moment stored away in the library of your memory, ask yourself if it was really worth it, and if it still means as much to you now as it did then.

Competition is another way you can make yourself

unhappy without realising you are doing it. Life is not a competition, you are not here to compete with your friends or people you envy. We are individuals, with our own goals, priorities, and have our own lessons to learn, we should not look at what others have or do and try to better them. We should not see the world as a race to outdo each other. The only people we should be competitive with are ourselves, and that comes with a health warning. Competition has its place, but I think that is in the sporting world, and I have never really got that either, probably because I am not good at any sports!

It takes a lot of energy to live up to expectations, I'd save it for something more constructive if I were you. Thoughts have funny tendencies of snowballing out of control. The secret is to realise this and stop them becoming an avalanche.

4

High as a Kite – Man's Vices

♪ *A Team*, Ed Sheeran ♪

As shocking as this may sound, every person I have ever met from my generation has taken some form of drug, and that is no exaggeration. As I met friends of friends, attended festivals, and started clubbing I realised it would be very hard to find someone who hadn't dabbled in some type of illegal drug. Later in life I found myself asking why we were all trying to alter our states of mind and mess with our internal balance. I came to the conclusion that everyone who takes drugs (of any classification) is simply trying to fill a void. They turn to drugs or other substances to forget, or **temporarily** mask a problem or issue. I think people turn to drugs for one of these three reasons:

1. Through <u>peer pressure</u>

2. They are <u>trying to escape</u> from reality

3. To have a '<u>good time</u>'

Don't get me wrong, this Lost Key isn't just aimed at junkies and druggies, but anyone who has dabbled with drugs or has an addictive personality.

You can't use drugs to mask a problem, when you sober up the problem will still be there, and I imagine nine times out of ten it will be worse than before. We have to face problems head on, and by masking a problem with a temporary cure or distraction like drugs, that is all it will be – a **temporary** solution.

I have learned a valuable lesson from my own experiences that in life the easy option is not usually the right option. A *really* basic example is the washing up! One Friday some time ago I left my dirty dishes on the side because I was going out to meet some friends. I left it all weekend and when, on Monday, I finally stopped putting it off it was such hard work! – The rice was stuck on like glue, and it was as if the saucepans were covered in concrete, but if I'd done them there and then it could have been so much easier. If you deal with the issues you are running from it will be so much easier for you in the long term.

The Three Types

1. For those that have taken drugs through so called 'peer pressure' it should be easier for you to escape the habit as you don't have any reason to carry on, you just have an addiction to a substance. The basic question to remember is that **you didn't need drugs when you were younger, so why do you need them now**? If you ask yourself this question enough times it will make you aware that your addiction is pointless.

2. Many kids and people of my generation are using drugs as a form of escape. Escape from the life that is presented to them. We are subjected to enormous amounts of pressure, change, information, and viewpoints on a daily basis. Instead of accepting the simple truths of both our inner and outer universes, we are trying to ignore them, and are changing our state of mind so we no longer have to deal with it all. I think the majority of 'users' fall into this category, but at this moment in time they are probably not aware of this underlying reason.

3. Then there are those who turn to drugs to have a good time – which I think is the reasoning for most people. In this case I think it's a poor excuse for trying to fill a void. If you are taking drugs to have a good time what does that say about you as a person? Most people experiment with drugs when they are younger, but the key is to become

aware of what you are doing and not get caught up in the easy roller coaster that is drug abuse. If you really think you need drugs in order to have a good time then it shows you are not yet aware of who you are.

Every drug has a side effect including the "soft" drugs such as Cannabis. Cannabis Psychosis occurs in the longer-term users, especially those who started young and before their brains were fully developed. Paranoia sets in, and the mind does not function as it should. I dabbled for a while, and I know that I was definitely developing a slight form of paranoia, and as soon as this realisation hit me I stopped smoking. Something that started as fun, full of giggles, and munchies, soon showed its negative side effects, and when I experienced them I knew I had to stop. I had to fill my void with something else.

I have met naïve people who say that Cannabis is simply grass, created by 'God', which makes it natural, but they are slightly bending the truth with that statement. The "natural" state is altered with some crazy man-made chemicals that weren't around in the days of hippies and free love, and this "natural grass" was not meant for inhalation.

I have come into contact with people who claim to use it as a form of escapism and a method of stilling the mind. This sounds like a poetic or bohemian justification, but there are other techniques that don't involve altering your mood with what can only be described as mind-altering chemicals.

I have experimented with various types of drugs

during my teenage years so I know first hand what it can do to a person. My justification was to have a good time, to drink from the cup of life and to try everything once. On reflection, if I am brutally honest with myself I did it for a good time and then ended up using it as a form of escapism while filling a void in my life. The common reasons for most people I would imagine.

On one occasion my best friend Thom, his brother Dan and his friend Dan all came to my studio flat in Stockwell in London for the weekend. We brought some Magic Mushrooms from Camden Market when they were legal (due to a loophole in the law). We scoffed the whole packet of mouldy, rank looking mushrooms within an hour, and after about thirty minutes we were all rolling around the flat laughing hysterically. I felt waves rush through my body every couple of minutes; I felt like the ocean one minute and a still pond the next. As the effects intensified the hysteria got worse. I thought, although I could have easily imagined it, that Thom's face had ballooned into a swollen red beetroot. Then we all began to calm down and question what was real in our own heads. Everything felt strangely false; the people, the studio flat I called home, and the only thing we were sure about was the rain outside the window. Everything we had once felt sure of was dissolved away in an instant. We rang my other best friend Helen and apparently made no sense whatsoever; she thought we were dying. The whole thing lasted for four *long* hours and the other Dan who had not eaten any (sensible guy) said it was the worst four hours of his life. He maintains to this day that we were like children in a mental institute who had lost their minds. Our faces seemed etched with uncertainty and we looked petrified at everything we caught sight of. For days afterwards I felt I had left a part of myself in that 'trip'. I was left with an empty feeling, questioning all of reality. It wasn't long after this experience that I came across that first spiritual book that put me on the path I am still on to this day.

On another occasion in Amsterdam, Thom, Helen and I crawled into McDonalds after visiting a load of Coffee Shops – funnily enough, not one drop of coffee touched our lips in those cleverly named drug dens – and I ordered EIGHT cheeseburgers. The lady behind the counter dutifully placed the eight cheeseburgers neatly onto a tray, clearly used to the antics of stoned tourists with the munchies. I paid, my left eye slightly shut (thanks to the effects of the weed), and then picked them all up individually, loading them into my arms, one on top of the other creating a wobbling tower effect. We were all laughing absolutely hysterically and Thom had tears rolling down his cheeks, I was totally oblivious and didn't really get why they were laughing so much. I thought it was perfectly natural at the time, it wasn't until the story was brought up the next day that I realised how out of my mind I had been. It was a scary realisation that a substance can dictate your actions, right down to the simple act of ordering food.

More importantly than my own weird and varied experiences with drugs, I have also seen the effects of drug abuse on close friends. Over a short period of time I saw their mood change, and I noticed that instead of making them happier, it actually had the reverse effect.

They ended up living for the next fix, with their life revolving around highs and lows. It completely altered their stability of mind and at the same time created problems in every part of their life due to paranoia and a lack of ability to function in social situations. They were a fraction of the person they used to be, which for me was very hard to watch.

With one person in particular the change was so dramatic that I felt the need to write a letter so they would realise their addiction and snap out of it. The letter I wrote was hard-hitting and very honest. Unfortunately, or fortunately, depending on how you look at it, the letter was found by her Mum!! I still bite my hand when I remember her telling me that! (eek). I barely recognised the person in question, after only one month of her using Cannabis, her emotional state had completely changed and her next Bong was more important than spending time with me or even eating. Luckily due to a change in her environment, circumstances, state of mind and much concern from friends, she cut down. I saw the withdrawal process first hand. I initially thought it's only Cannabis, how hard could it be to get 'clean'? But the readjustment to a drug free existence was very apparent. When she first stopped smoking she was at a loose end, and seemed like a "cat on a hot tin roof" – to quote a very apt saying. She couldn't seem to fill that initial void that had been temporarily covered up with drugs.

Everyone experiences this void if they don't have some kind of spiritual belief. It usually appears when you stop busying yourself with daily tasks or trivial preoccupations like TV. Often confused with boredom or a feeling of anxiety. This void cannot be filled with drugs. You need a clear head and the ability to control yourself and emotions **naturally, not chemically**! In some of the other Lost Keys I will share some examples to achieve this.

Our bodies were simply not designed to cope with huge alterations in emotions. What goes up must come down as they say! This metaphor is very true, with ecstasy in particular, for every high there is a low, or a "come down" as it is called by the chemical generation. Like everything in this world, there has to be a **balance**. Every person who takes drugs will reach a point where they take stock and realise that it is not giving them what they want. They begin to realise they are **empty, back at square one, questioning what they are doing with their life**.

Not only are your mind, body, and those around you affected by your drug abuse, so are the people that supply it or produce it. Revenue generated from drugs directly or indirectly funds other illegal activity such as human trafficking, prostitution, violent crimes and even murder. Too many users (and you are a 'user' even if you just dabble with drugs at the weekend) only think about their needs and don't give the rest of the process a second thought. It is a very selfish and naïve attitude to have – this only adds to the countless reasons why drugs should be a no go, or kicked out of your life as soon as possible.

If you actually think about all the chemicals and substances in any drug, it can do nothing but ruin your body, and you certainly can't claim that it's doing you any good! You have one body so look after it. It is a gift, as is your mind. Again, think back to when you were a child, perhaps around the age of twelve or so, you didn't need drugs to have a good time then, so what changed? **We must stop searching for happiness through external means. Happiness is inside of us, as it was when we were carefree children.**

Your mind is a powerful tool that should be treated like any other physical part of your body. Look after it. By simply stilling the mind and emptying it of all worries, problems, and questions, you can control an overactive mind easily *(see The Lost Key on Chilling and Zoning Out).*

You can turn over a new leaf at anytime in your life, no matter what you have done. All you need is the motivation to do it. These substances that so many people pump into their body are designed to give some kind of high to get you hooked. But if you want to give it up you can, it's all in the mind. There have been countless cases of people who have kicked Heroin and Crack, if they can give up the most addictive substances in the world then I am damn sure others can give up the less addictive ones.

An old house mate of mine once said to me "I know there is a stop button Tophy, (one of my nicknames) but I cant seem to find it yet" – I thought this was an amazingly simple but true statement, and it sums up my idea that everyone reaches a point of contemplation, takes a step back and realises enough is enough. The trouble is so many people have this feeling but then dismiss it, or try to block it out and end up back on drugs. The strong ones however, accept this feeling and hit that stop button with all their might.

I am glad I have experimented with drugs as it taught me the importance of lowering my inhibitions and knowing my emotional limits. Most importantly it taught me that everything has an equal and opposite reaction. It also showed me how lost people can become, how easily they throw their lives away to numb the pain of past experiences, and the unknown, how it takes away all stability from their life, and how it can ruin friendships and family relationships.

For anyone using drugs while reading The Lost Keys, you cannot expect to gain much from this book unless you have a clear mind – just think about the points above and actually wise up to the reality that drugs are not the way forward, no matter how "positively" they affect you for that **short** period of time. Give them up now before it's too late and you lose too much. As much as it might seem like fun and games now, I can assure you it will not continue. You will destroy yourself and lose those around you if you continue to take drugs. If you need any more encouragement or reasons to give up then just type 'drug addict' into a picture search engine on the internet!

To end on a slightly lighter note about drugs, my Mum who has never touched recreational drugs in her life had an interesting experience on Christmas Day not so long ago. She was on the drug called Zyban, which she was taking to help her quit smoking before the New Year. We had our usual Christmas Day feast, consisting of the mandatory thirteen vegetables, three types of stuffing to accommodate the vegetarians, and the usual Crimbo trimmings. After we had eaten, some of us dozed off in front of the fire, while others laughed hysterically at the Christmas comedy special on TV.

A few hours passed and Mum said she felt really tired and was going to take a nap. Soon after she called Vicky (my older sister). This quickly developed into an ambulance arriving as Mum couldn't breathe, felt dizzy, and was unable to move her limbs, she thought she had suffered a stroke. They arrived – ventilated her, and put it down to the Zyban, explaining it had the ability to create the side effects she was experiencing. Not long after they left, Simon (my older brother) told me he had put skunk – a strong form of cannabis – in the vegetarian stuffing again. "Again?" I asked, "What do you bloody mean again?" He said he had spiked the stuffing before, but no one had ever noticed. Turns out this particular year 'guzzle guts Mum' had pretty much polished off the whole lot by herself!! A few years later we told her the real reason for her funny turn and we all laughed about it. But she still swears she has never felt so out of control and lost in all her life. An interesting statement from a first time (unknowing) user don't you think? Needless to say Simon is banned from preparing the vegetarian stuffing, and it explains why we all used to nap and laugh so much after Dinner. Poor Granny still doesn't know to this day!

Booze

I am a self-confessed binge drinker, but I challenge you to find someone who lives in London at my age who isn't. That doesn't make it right, it's just a fact, and a scary one at that. The UK in particular is known for its drinking problems. My social life practically revolves around drink, pubs and clubs. The urban family and I have reigned it in a bit, but for a good three years it was not unusual, especially at Christmas, to find myself out three nights a week, then Friday and Saturday night, with the occasional 'red wine Sunday' thrown in for good measure. Each night would involve varying amounts of drink and levels of drunkenness, but I dread to think how much I have spent on the 'sauce' in my lifetime, or for that matter what state my liver is in.

As I have already said, balance is the key in all aspects of life, and if there is one thing in my life since becoming spiritual I have struggled with the most, it is creating a balance between my social/ drinking life and my spiritual life. It has been the hardest thing for me to make sense of. Buddha didn't tell us how to live life within a city of sin and distractions, he chilled out under a tree.

So the life of two halves – being a party animal and a spiritual person has divided me for a long time. I balanced drinking alcohol with eating healthy food, drinking buckets of water in the daytime, taking Milk Thistle (which is good for liver repair), and following my spiritual beliefs and thoughts involving meditation, yoga etc. I also regularly asked myself why I drank so much on nights out, I wanted to make sure I wasn't covering up any emotional pain or hurt that I hadn't dealt with. The answer was always the same; I wasn't, and I was just a product of my times, it was my generation's way of letting off steam, having fun and relaxing.

My Gran went to the cinema or for walks in the

woods to do the same thing. The NetGen as I call it (Internet Generation) needs more than that, because we are subjected to a thousand more distractions and stressful situations than my Gran ever was, and as sad as it is to say this, its just a cultural thing. One of my most recent housemates, a lovely guy named Kevin from Canada was with us for a year, and he soon learnt that the Brits culture is to binge drink, or just drink a lot. He spent many nights trying to catch-up with us, until a celeb-themed party crowned his mastery of the Brit culture once and for all. Dressed as Miranda from The Devil Wears Prada, and in exceptionally painful high heels that probably fuelled his intake of alcohol, Kevin was last seen pitching in his sunglasses screaming, "Get me Emily, EMILYYYYY". He went back to his motherland and found it hard to adjust to their drinking culture, or lack of it!

There is a fine line between a social drinker and an alcoholic, and as long as you are grounded, know your limits, and why you are doing what you are doing, then your days of being an alcoholic are far far away. One of the reasons I took myself off to India in 2012 was to make sure I wasn't trying to kid myself.

Friends, or people that have 'heard' of me will tell you I have a rep for being a socialite and party animal, which is kind of worrying, and I hope that doesn't stem from the fateful New Years Eve back in 2000 (still no Bacardi have touched these lips FYI!). I was glad to find out from my sojourn to foreign climes that my contemplations about drink were correct. I was safe. It was simple really, I just need to balance balance balance. I will drink when

I want (within reason and not at the crack of dawn), have fun with my dear friends and urban family and enjoy what is on offer. I know my priorities in life, and what is important to me, which I hope you are picking up on. Drink doesn't change my mental state, I don't get depressed from it, I am not using it to cover something up, and the amount of water I sneak down my gullet on nights out doesn't allow for hangovers and hopefully less liver damage. I am a binge-drinking spiritual guy from the NetGen, what more can I say?

5
Part 1

Second by Second – Living in the Present

♫ *Imagine*, John Lennon ♫

*L*IVE IN THE 'NOW' OF every experience is what most of the New Age books keep telling me to do. For a while I didn't understand what they meant, but now I realise, and hope I can relay it clearer than I could have done in those early years! We need to live in the 'now' of each moment, it is a great way to unlock one of the doors to happiness. A prime example of living in the now is one of my friends who travelled round the world with me on a three-week holiday (as crazy as that sounds). He was so excited about getting to each destination, then when he arrived I noticed he seemed disappointed, and on occasions miserable. It occurred to me that he might be looking at these places as potential sources of happiness, each new destination as a remedy for unhappiness. When the destinations didn't meet his expectations he ended up looking forward to the next trip, and at each destination he ended up in the same emotional state as before, if not worse because he felt deflated each time. Why compare to the past, or wish for the future, why can't we just enjoy the moment – <u>the present</u>?

You can travel anywhere, meet anyone, but if you're looking elsewhere to get your emotional gauge to full you will never know the true meaning of being happy and content. I bet money that if you took a chronically depressed person to Mauritius they would be just as unhappy there as they would be in their hometown once the initial novelty wore off. I am not saying that you can't find happiness from some external sources, of course you can, but it doesn't compare to owning your own plentiful supply, and that's why you don't need to rely on chemical fixes, other people, environments, or experiences. A truly happy individual is as happy in their own company as they are in a group, or as happy spending a rainy day in London as they are on a beach in Australia.

This internal happiness does not appear overnight, and is something that takes work and effort. I feel I am now at a point where I have found an internal happiness that is unshakeable, still some way to go, but unshakeable. It took time, but I now have it because of the disciplines I have put into practice over the years, such as the lifestyle

I lead, the lessons I have learnt, experiences I have put myself in, my viewpoints, control over my mind, and generally the belief systems I follow that are outlined in this book. Not so long ago, when I was back in The Shire (my hometown), Laura my sister was winding me up saying (with a coy smile) "Is Chrissy in a little bit of a bad mood, is he unhappy? Is he, is he?" I realised, as I perhaps wasn't my usually bubbly self that I must have come across as unhappy. But I simply said to her that I no longer get bad moods or feel unhappy anymore. I just have reflective moods that might appear that way. As I said it I thought; "f*ck me, I really don't have bad moods or negative feelings anymore, when did that happen!?" I couldn't remember the transition, and I found it hard to recall what it actually felt like to feel unhappy. I knew exactly why – I found happiness within me and nothing or no one can take that away from me. I am content and live in the now. In that instant I also knew that it is attainable for every single person on this planet.

And I must point out that being happy doesn't mean laughing and smiling all the time. You can be happy inside without having to show it by laughing hysterically and putting on a fake smile. Sometimes the happiest people are those who say little compared to those that command a room.

By living each moment for what it is, we do away with **comparison** and **expectations** that only lead to feelings of unhappiness. These two words that I have highlighted can be huge sources of unhappiness so do away with them as soon as you can.

If you are living in the now and experiencing everything

as it happens you wont miss a thing. I went to New Years Eve 07/08 at the London Eye, next to the River Thames and as the bells on Big Ben began to strike twelve to welcome in the New Year and the fireworks launched into the sky, almost 90% of the entire crowd whipped out their mobile phones and started filming or taking pictures!! The scene turned into an ocean of tiny video screens bobbing in the air, and I was standing there looking through these one-inch squares asking myself what the hell they were doing. I appreciate a picture or video as much as the next person, 5000 pictures on my Facebook will tell you that, and I was glad we got some pictures of the event, but there comes a point when you need to know when a visual picture means more than a photographic one. I was just soaking it all up, every tiny second at a time. I was pretty hammered by then, but appreciated it for what it was; a visual treat to my eyes, and I could see everything in panoramic view without the restriction of a tiny electronic screen. My memory was my camera, and with that picture I also took in all of the senses that I experienced including the dongs of Big Ben and the amazing lucid colours of the fireworks. I feel that I experienced that moment in its entirety compared to the rest of the crowd.

By looking forward or backwards in any situation you will often miss the moment you should be experiencing. I know people who have backpacked in Australia and come back to the UK saying that their trip was rubbish. This was probably because they were just living for the next experience, the next town, or the next country on their long list of adventures and comparing it to the last place. What a waste, and what an expensive time warp. They look back on their travels and realise that even in those moments of what they considered boredom, there was something to be experienced. I have been around the globe both with work and privately. With work I visited Portugal for three hours, and Perth in Australia for a weekend. But I find that is all you need, I like a city or country, not by its architecture necessarily or any hype surrounding it, but by a feeling I get. If you are living in the moment then you will notice these feelings more and more.

I am on a holiday in Australia as I write this section, visiting Laura and her boyfriend Steve in Cairns who are doing just that – travelling, and we have just returned from a trip to somewhere called Cape Tribulation. We spent about five hours getting to 'Cape Trib' as the gorgeous Aussie people call it, travelling along the North East coast of Australia. On the left side of the road was a high sloping rainforest and on the right side miles of unspoilt sandy beaches. Some of the people on the bus went straight to sleep with the intention of only waking up at the destination, but I considered the whole journey as part of the adventure and I saw some of the most spectacular sights that quite simply took my breath away. I couldn't stop smiling the whole way, and if anyone had caught a glimpse of me they would have probably said I was high on drugs or had just escaped from a mental asylum! Once upon a time before air travel, people who were privileged enough to travel considered the journey as part of the trip. I think that is really important thing to remember, even if you are cooped up in economy class, with the seat in front crushing your kneecaps and a ten-hour stretch ahead of you.

I am currently sitting cross-legged on the floor of a wooden balcony about 15ft wide, open to the elements with no windows in the quirky Victorian hostel we are staying in. It is the type of place you can picture an old man smoking a pipe in his wooden rocking chair after a day working at the gold mine. It's been raining heavily most of the day, and that strange indescribable smell of rain is hanging in the air. I can see the lush tropical environment ahead of me, the clouds are reaching down from the sky and practically tickling the treetops of the mountainside which looks truly incredible. I feel as if I want to run up the mountainside and be engulfed by its sheer beauty, letting my Spirit be absorbed into the environment. Every second I live I aim to experience it in that second. By doing so, it literally changes your entire outlook on time and the importance of each precious moment we are given.

When I am truly living in the now it seems as if I am in sync with the Universe and everything contained in it. This feeling is earth shattering and something I hope everyone will experience when they are ready to. It gives you such a deep connection to everything around you that you instinctively know you have found the right path to happiness. The past is important as we learn from it. The future is vital so we can plan our path and know where we are headed, as without direction we cannot reach a destination. However, the focus of our attention should not be the past or future but the present moment. With this outlook you will begin to see the benefits unfold very quickly.

5
Part 2

Mother Nature & You Time – Living in the Present

♪*Colours Of The Wind, Pocahontas (Disney)* ♪

The lease expired on one of my flats in London before I had managed to find another one – a mistake I won't repeat in a hurry. During this time I was technically homeless and after a month of sofa-surfing I found myself living with my best friend Helen in Surrey for two months. I was speaking to her about one of my train journeys back to her house from London, and I was saying that I just loved the natural beauty of the world. I gave her the example of the canal and fields that

I passed on the train every evening after work, with the sun radiating through the gaps in the trees. She said she didn't really notice things like that – which I found surprising. Then it dawned on me that some people probably just look where they are walking and not at the bigger picture surrounding them every single day. I have had some inspiring experiences with Mother Nature, she has shown me the most beautiful sights and now lets me see the beauty in all things. These magic moments happen more frequently once you begin to learn to live in the present.

If you have ever been to a beach or the top of a hill and had that awe inspiring feeling that makes you think "wow" this is truly beautiful, then you will know what I mean. You can feel totally invigorated and uplifted if you just "breathe-in" the beauty of these natural surroundings and know that wherever you are in the world there is always beauty to be seen. I think it's really important to open up your field of vision and take in all of natures creations, I find it helps put things into perspective.

I have taken a very similar route to work for the last nine years. I walk through St James's Park at least three times each week. Every single time I notice new things, or see the scene in a different light. It might be a squirrel collecting nuts, new blossom on a tree, or how the rain makes patterns on the lake. It's not until you think about how amazingly complex these simple and stunning creations are, and how they fit into the grand plan that you take away a deep found appreciation for the world and how we all have our own place within it. It also helps to respect the natural planet and realise our actions directly effect our surrounding environment – climate change is a perfect example!

Every creature in its natural habitat has an important role in the circle of life. It directly affects the life of another creature. Plants and trees are also a part of something much bigger than themselves, everything in nature is there for a reason and when I see a squirrel collecting nuts I think that I am so lucky to be able to appreciate that as much as I appreciate mankind's existence. An invisible thread connects everything in the natural world and one snip can cause big problems. When we mess with nature we open up a time bomb that is guaranteed to explode. Respect for our planet and the natural environment is very important to our own life, and our very survival counts on our natural world remaining as it was once created.

I used to drive on car journeys and then realise I couldn't remember the last ten minutes of the drive, which just proved that I wasn't living in the "now" and my mind was elsewhere. Too many people just concentrate on the basic task of getting to their destination in their imaginary three-foot square box of personal space, but it doesn't take much to look ahead of you, to the side, and above, to begin to appreciate what is on this planet and realise what you are a part of. You'll be amazed at the amount of things that go on around you, and with time, I am sure it will bring you a better understanding of where you fit into the jigsaw of life, and an understanding that the human race is not superior to anything else in our world. I walk about like a kid exploring a new maze or forest, my eyes are looking at everything, noticing, evaluating, loving and appreciating.

Avatar is now my favourite film, but I say that about every new film I see that hits me on a deep level, so I should say my favourite film of the moment – and it dawned on me that most fantasy films all have trees involved somewhere in their story-lines. The trees possess certain spiritual qualities, contain ancient magic and an age-old wisdom. I believe this is by no mere coincidence. The hippy movement were often labelled tree huggers, but taking that seriously for a moment, there is an element of truth and reality behind hugging trees. Try not to smirk as you read on! I remember visiting one of my Mum's spiritual friends, Carol, when I was ten years old. She had a lovely old cottage, surrounded by landscaped gardens backing onto a clear flowing stream. One of the rooms in her house was dedicated to healing and I apparently used to call it the "Magic Special Room". One sunny afternoon these two New Age ladies took me into the garden, down beside the stream underneath a huge ancient sprawling Willow tree. They told me "look up from the trunk towards the sky and imagine how many things this tree had seen changing over the hundreds of years it had been alive. The changing of the environment, the change in soil nutrients, the weather, the people who have walked near it, the generations of families, the whispers of human conversation, the collective human thought processes evolving over the years." They went on to explain the importance of this tree to our very existence. Carol and Mum said to hug a tree and pour love into it would result in this tree returning the same love back to us, but magnified ten-fold.

We stretched our arms round the huge trunk and in my view performed a long forgotten ritual of loving nature in all its magnificent, mysterious glory. This was truly an uplifting moment for me and from what I can remember it felt as if the Willow was breathing a life force into my very Spirit. Filling me up with the suns energy, the world's wisdom, a life force, and that all-encompassing love that is abound in the universe. Appreciation of nature will lead you rapidly to happiness and help you to learn more about yourself. We all originate from the times when we lived in absolute harmony with the Earth as the natives did in Avatar, and in a way we still do. Our homes are all made from the elements and materials we have found on this planet, but we have just evolved in a way that takes us away from the physical beauty of nature.

That is what we must return to, a way of experiencing nature in its entirety, by getting out there into the wild even if its just a local park and feeling the magic of our naturally occurring environment. I love just listening to the wind rustle the trees, I take a deep breath and then blow out with the wind as it commands the leaves, trees and plants to move. Soak it up, there is so much to get from the simplicity of nature – go get yourselves connected.

One thing I really miss in London – that I loved when living in the countryside, is the view of the stars. In London they are almost entirely obscured by light pollution. I love looking up into the night sky and imagining the endless possibilities, life-forms, existences, distances, time-spans and the wonders it offers. Shooting stars take my breath away as fireworks once did when I was a kid. I think the beauty of stars also includes a certain amount of mystery that makes me feel part of something much bigger than the "Me" who works nine to five in order to survive. Have you ever looked up at the stars and just wondered why? What is up there? How big is the Universe? Why are we here, at this moment in time, on a planet that is millions of years old? How the hell can Earth be the only Planet in the whole of the Universe to house intelligent beings, a Universe that is so big we cannot even begin to calculate its continually growing dimensions?

The odds were stacked against us right from the first spark of the Big Bang, and it is worth contemplating that we are incredibly lucky to even exist as a Planet, let alone as a species. The series of events leading from the Big Bang to the evolution of man was incalculably impossible, full of luck and chance so I understand it. It is nothing short of a miracle that we exist in our current state, a change of one or two degrees in temperature during an Ice Age could have prevented our evolution altogether. This realisation is so huge, but also truly humbling, and forces me to appreciate my surroundings more than ever before.

I am currently sat on the Eurostar from Brussels (another work trip) to Waterloo as I type this, and although this may sound hypocritical, everyone around me is using some form of electronic device to amuse themselves. I continually have moments where I feel I have to look at the countryside around me. I think I have just entered France and the scenery to my left and right is incredible. The sun is setting over the trees on top of a hill in the distance, cows are grazing, and the only sign of civilisation is a little run down French shack near the top of a hill. Looking up at the sky, I can see huge white fluffy clouds and shards of sunlight are piercing through them like some sort of spiritual painting from the renaissance period.

As important as appreciating nature is, so is appreciating every single human being on this planet. There is no point in seeing the beauty of the world around us if we cannot see the magic within us and within others. I believe we inhabit a world that is beyond scientific explanation or words, it is a place that has infinite possibilities, infinite views, infinite experiences, and infinite encounters; it is a place where we can all find beauty, and a sense of purpose, if we begin to look at the world with our New Age minds switched on.

Since I have been on this train, not one person has looked up and appreciated their surroundings. Actually, the only time they have looked up was when we stopped at 'Lille Europe Station'! They are all too pre-occupied with their temporary fixes and distractions. Their DVD players, their mobile phones, their Blackberries, their hand-held computer games. It just struck me that not one of the twelve people in this carriage are just "enjoying" their journey, they all seem as if they're trying to kill time before reaching their destination. It's almost as if they were wishing away their time. I know that in the western world time seems to be slipping away from us because of added pressures from our jobs, but the use of time should be prioritised as much as possible. We each only have **one single chance** on this planet and I don't know about you, but I have begun to notice that time moves much faster as I grow older so all the more reason to use it wisely. We all need to make the most of each moment, and not wish away precious hours with materialistic distractions.

After seeing an old rusty plough next to a shed a moment ago I started to daydream about the time before the invention of the technical gadgets that surround me at the moment. My grandparents, and even my Mum did not have any of the technology being used on this train when they were my age, and it's interesting to see that when they meet complete strangers – usually of a similar age group to themselves – they happily chat away and try to get to know each other, find things in common, and generally befriend each other. Without needing to rely heavily on the distractions of the modern world, they use one of their basic human instincts; interaction with those around them. I think by listening and talking to other people, and by discovering their opinions and beliefs you grow, learn, and develop as a person. You will begin to see that you 'bump' into the right people at the right time. It is like an overall plan, the secret is to ask the right questions so you receive the answers you are looking for. I know that we're **all** here to help each other grow as individuals. Regardless of age, religion, race and sex. By simply interacting when you can, you move forward a step in your quest for greater unity and happiness.

To me this is still the hardest thing I am learning as I find it difficult to strike up conversations with random strangers but think it will come with more inner confidence, and will become easier with practice and time. And as I feel so strongly about interacting with those who I come into contact with, I will continue to push myself until it becomes natural or part of my nature.

Although I am writing on my laptop and attempting to explain the down sides of technology abuse, I wish I could just log off and sit back and soak up the rolling fields of France and the flocks of birds that I just caught sight of. Since starting my new job this is the first chance I have had both the time and the energy to add more to this book, so instead of soaking up the scenery or interacting with the other people on this train I am choosing to write more in my attempt at prioritising. You have to prioritise according to your lifestyle, but the point I want to make is this; we all have to realise the importance of living each moment, appreciating nature, and learning from, and interacting with, the people who cross our paths.

Your spiritual improvement is more important than anything else. I know spirituality is the route to happiness and has the power to answer all those innate questions we share, and has the power to make all dreams come true. Surely this is priority number one for all of us.

As well as appreciating nature and interacting with those around you, another thing that helps us grow as individuals is the use of our ability to still our minds and have "you time". In a typical life where you work nine-five, Monday – Friday, you have your own property (rented or bought), friends, family, a car, loads of red tape and things to deal with, you will have bills to pay, stress at work, stress at home, time to manage between work, home, and friends, and the (hopefully) not so frequent problems like bad health, and family or relationship issues. That is why it is so important to set aside time to still your over-active mind.

Without much thought we go to sleep every night and rest our bodies, and to some degree rest our minds, but I think we could all spend time resting our minds more completely.

The lifestyles led by people five hundred years ago would not have created so much stress or pressure on their time as we now experience, and if we go back even further in time those people would have led much less complicated lives. Yet the majority of us still need to learn how to deal, spiritually and mentally, with the amazing but rapid way in which our race has evolved in such a relatively short period of time. I don't think we are mentally capable of dealing with the revelations that have come about in the 21st century. We have all been swept up by these developments with the force of a hurricane, and in the process we have forgotten what is important to us. We now need to deal with these changes on a **much deeper level**.

6

Chilling & Zoning Out – Meditating

♪ *Slip Into Something More Comfortable*, Kinobe ♪

*L*IVING IN THE 21ST CENTURY sometimes feels like we are swimming in a vast Ocean, always swimming at great speed towards some unknown destination. Meditation is the equivalent of finding a large piece of driftwood that you can climb onto, relax and take a break from the struggle of staying afloat. The dangers in the Ocean such as sharks and storms are mere distractions similar to the technological 'advances' we are surrounded by. We need the driftwood, the meditation, to contemplate, to still our minds, to take a break and look inwardly so we can discover our individual destinations.

Fifty years ago people thought of meditation as a Buddhist monk in a far away place sitting crossed legged in a cave, but with the shrinking of the world and sharing of information it is now very popular with westerners and practiced globally by all types of people. It is an excellent method of stilling the mind. Scientists are studying the process of controlled breathing and focusing the mind, and are discovering the many positive benefits meditation can produce. It's good for the heart, it helps reduce stress levels and blood pressure, and promotes good mental health. The few people I know who meditate do not have anxiety attacks or similar issues, they just radiate calmness and tranquility.

I have never understood why people experience anxiety or panic attacks. I just can't see why they let themselves feel like that. Helen (my best friend) has more of a scientific approach to these types of questions. She flipped this little thought of mine on its head and said that it's something these people cannot control, they can't help the way they react. To a certain degree, I guess I agree with her – if you don't have full control over your body and thoughts then this type of disorder is uncontrollable, but I know you can change who you are and how you react to situations only if **you** want to – and countless spiritual people, Psychiatrists and Counselors will tell you the same thing. You have the power to control all aspects of the person you are – or wish to become, but no-one else can do it for you. By saying that you can't control your feelings or thought processes you are just refusing to accept self-responsibility. If you suffer from these attacks you can control them through meditation.

You don't have to be a monk, or sit for hours to meditate. You can do as little or as much as you like, from sitting by yourself for a while, to counting from one to ten, or practice every day for thirty minutes in a quiet place. By regularly taking the time to go somewhere quiet and free from distraction, as you would take time to eat or sleep, you can still your mind and relax. I try and do this three times a week. I meditate in a quiet room where I feel safe and secure. I sit down in a position that I find comfortable (not like the many images you see of spiritual masters sat cross- legged with their hands in some lotus position!) but not too comfortable as I have found myself falling flat on my face dribbling and snoring. Sometimes I light incense sticks to add to the mood and the scent helps my focus.

I first started meditating by sitting in the middle of my bedroom floor with the lights out staring into a single candle flame. This allowed me to focus on one thing, and if any other thoughts entered my mind I tried to shift them aside and return to concentrating on that single flickering flame. I had no expectations of what the meditation would do for me, a key factor I think. After a while the most bizarre sensation occurred, I became the flame of the candle. I was aware of my body but my mind or spirit was now with the candle flame and I was objectively looking at my body as a mere shell. My inner and outer world became a single flickering flame in a darkened room. To bring all your thoughts back to that one image is a very humbling feeling that simplifies your life and lets you see what is important against the backdrop of a busy materialistic world.

Silence always tells the truth, and that is why most people will never allow themselves to be surrounded by utter silence. How many of you can remember the last time you were in total silence, without distraction of music, TV, books, or visual stimulation? ...and sleeping doesn't count!! Give it a go, and if, when you have your eyes closed you hear the fridge beginning to hum, birds chirping, thinking about what you had for breakfast that morning, or if that guy or girl will ever call you back, bring it to your attention, and then move it out of your mind. Just be aware of what is going on in your head and deal with it slowly. Anything that flits into your head when you start the process should be moved out, notice it, don't associate it as negative or positive and just let it go and don't "answer" it with another thought!

I sometimes wonder if we are scared of being alone without our technological distractions. In my lifetime, say between 1990 and 2012, I am shocked to see how much change I have lived through. Take the simple mobile phone for example – how it went from a large brick, to a phone with a greenish screen and the luxury of having a game called Snake, then it could take photos, then the option of touch screen, then internet on phones changed everything, and Wi-fi pushed the boundaries even further. Now my phone can do more than my battered old laptop, and with a simple swipe it can pay for food in shops. We have the Ipad, 3D TVs (I still remember my black & white box of a TV), electronic books, and the list goes on. Shit-a-brick, when will we get chance to take stock and evaluate these leaps in evolution? There is so much to distract us from….well, ourselves. **It's wrong, we need more balance, and we need to know when to leave all the gadgets and time-consuming distractions alone**. I am sure these distractions are one of the largest contributing factors to our feeling of being out of touch with ourselves, and the world. The solution is simple, get away from them for a while, if that's for thirty minutes a day, or ten minutes a week, it *will* help.

I once taught a Major in the British Army to meditate when I was working in Basra, Iraq. I wasn't a soldier, but was working as a Diplomat in the Consulate-General in Southern Iraq. We civilians (or 'civvies' as we were known) worked closely with the British Army and had a few Army folk working in our building, which made for a more interesting mix of people. The Major and I were at lunch one afternoon and he asked me how I always seemed so cheery and relaxed. I said it was probably because of my spiritual interests and that meditation really helped in difficult situations, especially in a war zone. *The Major*, as I came to call him, was a gentle giant, a lovely, jovial, funny, interesting and kind Glaswegian, and it wasn't long before he became a trusted friend of mine. He would tell endless funny stories and keep the mood light, as well as having the dual ability of being a fantastic listener. He asked if I could teach him meditation one night so I agreed on the proviso that he wore something comfortable and not his usual camouflaged uniform. I packed up some incense sticks, candles, calming Zen music, put on my body armour, helmet, walkie-talkie, and emergency first aid kit and walked over to his "Pod" (accommodation made out of a shipping container and concrete sand bags). I thought how bizarre it was to be walking with this New Age stuff while listening out for the usual whooshing sounds of rockets and mortars, ready to dive into the dirt at any moment.

The strangeness didn't end there, The Major opened his door to me in a full white Arab robe called a Dishdasha, we both laughed at the sight of him in native gear and me with my New Age supplies in full head-to-toe body armour. If only the UK press had snapped a picture! Once we had composed ourselves, I put on the music, sat on the floor and lit the candles and incense sticks and then I talked him through a basic meditation. I told him "breathe slowly, slower, relax every muscle and just look at the candle. Let your world drop away, all thoughts disappear, relax and breathe." I asked him to concentrate on the feeling of his breathe going in and out of his nose, and nothing else. I don't know how long we were there until the incoming rocket alarm sounded, alerting us that another rocket had been fired into our compound by the local insurgents, but he said it was an amazing experience, he felt calm, and had a feeling of serenity wash over him. At first his thoughts were running wild, going from one thought to another, but at some point he stopped fighting and they dropped away. If a Major in the Army can do it, I think anyone can.

The most basic explanation I have ever heard of meditating is **to just watch your thoughts, whatever they may be**. That's it, that's meditation in a nutshell.

With time, your mind will find it easier to switch off. It helps to have a quiet room, and preferably without impending rocket attacks, as this allows for complete inward focus. I use deep breathing, which helps to focus the mind and gives me a physical feeling of well-being and relaxation. The deep breathing also has a physiological effect; by taking larger quantities of oxygen around the blood stream, and eventually directly to the brain. By combining the deep breathing, focusing on one simple object (eventually nothing will be required), and being quiet and still in mind and body you can learn to relax and discipline your mind. You can also play relaxing music or chant to help you get to a state of relaxation. I think the key principle is that you are doing it to relax your mind. You should use whatever methods you find most comfortable, and don't worry about what you think you ought to be doing or experiencing. I no longer use a single focus to still my mind, I now simply focus on my breath, on the inhale and exhale and the slight feeling of the breath touching the place above the upper lip. Meditation acts as a kind of holiday for my mind. It's really hard to describe what I experience other than perfect peace and serenity, but I end up being part of that nothingness and devoid of myself.

Depending on what I want to experience during meditation I sometimes use visualisation and imagine being somewhere like a beach I have visited on holiday, or a mountaintop in Nepal and this gives me a "pick-me-up" sort of effect. These various forms of meditation will allow you to experience a balanced mental state while allowing you to switch off from the outside world. These techniques are natural processes that you can control, unlike the use of external stimulants like drugs (prescription or otherwise).

You will also find that whatever type of meditation you choose, the process helps you put things into perspective. You can meditate on a particular question by thinking of it as you begin the deep breathing process. By keeping that one and only thought in the back of your mind you will find the answers come to you with little or no effort, usually in the form of intuition or signs. These answers don't always come instantaneously, I have found the 'answers or signs' in a newspaper I picked up the next day, or on another occasion met someone a week later who began talking, quite out of the blue, about the very thing I had meditated on.

I believe meditation works because you have clarity of mind and absolute focus rather than that swirling mess your mind becomes when you're under pressure or stressed. Sometimes you hear people say "take some deep breaths and count to ten" – that is just a simple form of meditation!

Just as my body is allowed to rest when I am sleeping, meditation pushes all thoughts out of my overactive head, and gives my mind the rest it needs. Give it a try, take just a small piece of your day for **you**. There is no need to even call it meditation, just call it 'you time' or something. It might take a couple of attempts before you feel you have got the hang of it, but it will work, and it will help you. There are enough meditation classes or drop-in centres available if you want direct instruction or a group vibe.

I have only told two people about this in my life

but I feel I should share this to prove the enormous capability of the mind. When my older sister Vicki was really ill in hospital before she died, I was in Australia with my younger sister Laura and her boyfriend Steve. I was in Cairns, northern Australia by the Lagoon – a huge outdoor pool. It was boiling hot and a perfect day, I plugged in my Ipod and played my Zen meditation playlist. I zoned out, I wasn't there or anywhere really – it's a similar experience to when you are really tired and doze off in the sun, then you wake up and can't remember if you were asleep or not!

Anyway, as I was meditating on Vicki getting better, sending her positive thoughts and vibes, saying in my head "if you want another shot at life, you can do it, but only if *you* want to", I kept on getting this strong feeling that I needed to turn around, so my head was where my feet were and vice-versa. After I came to, I didn't think much of it but told my Mum on the phone about the experience and she said it was probably because I was in Australia, and upside down or 'down-under' so to speak. But when we got back to the UK after receiving the call to tell us Vicki had died, I was sitting in the lounge with Vicki's husband (my brother-in-law) and my Mum, she looked at him and said "go on Gian-Franco, tell him what happened" He looked at me with wide eyes and told me that the same night I had been meditating, Vicki had turned around in her bed, was agitated and wanted to lie the other way, virtually pulling the drips and plugs out of her arms to move!! Gob smacked doesn't really cover it guys, I felt a thousand pins and needles run down the back of my spine when he told me this, tears welled up in my eyes, and I felt very faint! I was scared of the power I had tapped into. That was no coincidence. I had telepathically picked up on her feelings from the other side of the world while in a state of pure relaxation and focus. That's proof, if ever there was, that this stuff actually works!

I was lucky enough to work in Burma for a month. It is a beautiful and very spiritual country. The majority of the population are Buddhists and meditate as regularly as we would watch TV. One evening I visited the Shewedagon Pagoda, the largest dedicated place of worship in the capital city. The Pagoda is made up of the main golden dome that can be seen from all over the city and the surrounding mass of mini pagodas. It took me ten minutes just to walk around the base of the dome. The pagoda is located just outside downtown Rangoon, and situated on a hill that allows for inspiring views before sunset, and minimal noise pollution from the city. As I walked bare-footed – slower than I have ever done before in my life – the constant tinkling of bells rang in my ears and filled my body with complete calmness. Gradually the monks, nuns, and ordinary locals started beating the 5ft high bells dotted around the dome with wooden beaters to create the perfect relaxation atmosphere, and some began a low chant that reverberated around the entire scene. Then, as if someone had turned on a tap above me, the heavens opened and the rain started to bucket down. At that point I didn't really care, I just continued walking with my bare feet sloshing around in the puddles and raised my head to the heavens, grateful to experience that moment for what it was. It was the monsoon season, so what's a boy to do I thought to myself!

Everyone was staring at me as if I was the first westerner they had ever seen, and yet they all smiled and took a triple look, and the few that spoke small amounts of English braved a "Hello, where you from Mr?" but the majority seemed in complete awe of me. "Is this what being a celebrity is like?" I pondered, then quickly snapped back to my current reality. One young monk of a similar age talked with me on my way out. He spoke lightning-fast broken English, and there was something about him that drew me in. I have **never ever** felt that way before when looking into someone's eyes. We stood on the steps and just looked into (not at) each other for what seemed like an eternity. It was an attraction, but not physical or emotional. This memory still sends goose bumps up my arms when I recall it, there was nothing there – just the two of us, encased in two bodies looking at each other on some other level. A simple magnetic attraction to a person, one that still escapes any words I can use to describe it. I have tried and tried, edited and deleted, paraphrased and elaborated, but try as I might I simply cannot find words to illustrate the feeling and emotion as I looked into the eyes of that saffron-robed, mysterious and loving, gentle young man. He touched my soul, and my higher self. Somehow, without communicating what I wanted to, I felt he knew anyway. I sent silent messages of peace and understanding to him as best I could. We went our separate ways, me into my waiting car, and him, shoeless, into the rain towards his monastery. Perhaps just two people, existing in two very different but parallel worlds.

I returned to the Pagoda most nights, I must admit I went there with the slight hope that I would see my saffron-robed friend again, but it wasn't meant to be. I still enjoyed walking around in my trance-like state, and sitting under the isolated mini pagodas just watching the serene environment of chanters, bell ringers, and people meditating. That place held a certain energy, which I put down to the mentality of those situated there; optimistic, positive, calm, loving, and simple. You could feel the energy in the air, in much the same way as you can feel the stress and panic at airports or when commuting.

While in Burma I was introduced to a very influential and enlightened Monk. He agreed to take me to his countryside monastery and teach me some insights. I had to hide in the back of the car under a blanket as we crossed a bridge and government checkpoints. He was taking me there at great personal risk to himself, and I could have been accused of spying or influencing an uprising if caught. Something told me it was worth the risk so I trusted my intuition (as we all should). We spent ten hours together, undercover from the Burmese Regime, and debated mind-expanding theories about the Universe. I still can't grasp some of the messages he imparted, but it made me certain that I am on the right path and therefore qualified and capable of sharing my lessons with the world. During our time together he taught me a new method of meditating which on return to the capital I began practicing every night.

He called it mindfulness. Now stay with me as I try

and describe this very advanced method. His technique was focused on trying to observe oneself objectively. Sitting quietly and observing 'you' as separate from body *and* mind – "to notice things, but not to notice you are noticing" he would drum into me. For example, if he was sitting on his foot for too long he would note the sensation, but neither try to ignore it or associate it as negative. It sounds very tricky but he best described it as letting the Spirit analyse the body and mind. This method is very powerful, but the teaching behind it should only be used and interpreted by those who are ready for the lessons. I believe his teachings and meditation techniques have the ability to catapult the spirituality of a person forward with huge speed, or send them barking mad and insane – depending on how far they have travelled on their spiritual path. His messages took my breath away and transformed my entire view on life in that one instant; more than I had originally thought possible.

I came away shell-shocked, as did my interpreter and friend, Sue (not her real name). Our late night car journey back to the city over potholes, through the police checkpoints and across rice fields was a confusing time for both of us. We kept on repeating the same line over and over – "nothing is real", and as soon as we both tried to verify his teachings by explaining it to each other we came unstuck and started laughing. It truly was life altering. "What about the sun then Sue?" I said, "Surely that is real?" She smiled and just said in a mock monk voice "ahhr, but this 'sun', it has been defined by humans as so, it is impermanent, there one minute, gone the next, it is no more real than you or I. Perceived by different people in different ways, constantly changing in its atomic make-up". Everything we came up with ended up being 'not real' – damn it, the unnamed Monk was right. It was like a game of trying to out-smart the teacher. We both laughed and then I fell into a deep daydream.

There was one thing the enlightened monk taught me that was very easy to understand, and this was in response to my question about what he thought the main cause of unhappiness was. After two minutes of silence (this was a normal gap I became accustomed to) he replied **"the mind"**, two minutes later he followed this with **"you only have negative experiences because you see them that way"**. I wanted to write a book and print only this phrase on each page as I believed in it so much.

It is **SO** true, if we in the western world could change our mindsets and see negative experiences in a different way, we could change our entire outlook on life, which would ultimately lead to a happier life. When a negative experience crosses your mind, turn it into a positive experience. My Mum broke her hip and couldn't drive two weeks before Vicki died and instead of seeing it as an inconvenience she felt it happened so that Vicki's husband had to take time off work and spend more time with her in hospital before she died.

The various forms of meditation I practice have developed my spiritual thinking and added so much to my character, personality and life. You can tell from just looking at a person if they meditate and are in touch with their spirituality. It radiates outwards from within just like that young monk I met on the steps of Shewedagon Pagoda (cue the goose bumps again).

Other techniques with similar benefits to meditation include Yoga, Tai Chi and Visualisation. All benefit the three things that make us human – the Mind, the Body, and the Spirit (or Soul). I do Yoga most mornings, and the more I read about Yoga the more I think it should be taught in all Physical Education classes in schools around the world. The postures not only tone the body but also directly affect the health of most of your organs, respiratory, and circulatory systems. Perhaps more importantly Yoga aids concentration, and focuses the mind. I believed in this so much that you could often find me doing Yoga in full body armour by the lake in Basra, Iraq. It really helped me keep a grip on reality while working in such hostile and claustrophobic conditions, although in hindsight it probably looked like I had lost my marbles to any unsuspecting passersby.

In London you can find numerous Hot Yoga studios that offer Yoga in rooms heated to aprox 37c, which helps you sweat more toxins and improves flexibility. I love it, and have introduced most of my urban family to the delights. Tai Chi has similar benefits but I find it more relaxing. Both are ways of connecting with the inner stillness we all possess, and the practices help to achieve a more balanced state of mind in this fast-paced environment we are subjected to. Massage is also a great way to unwind mentally, it can be expensive but it is worth every penny, and again helps to release toxins and stress. If I could afford it I would go once a week, for now I have to make do with being pummeled once a quarter.

Visualisation is another form of meditation. The idea is that you imagine and visualise a dream or outcome with absolute faith – feel it, smell it, be the dream, believe you can achieve it and it will manifest into reality. With encouragement from my Mum I used visualisation when I was at Primary School to overcome Glandular Fever. Every night she would guide me through a series of visualisations aimed at destroying the illness inside of me. The golden crystal I had chosen to help me destroy the disease broke in half rather mysteriously the same day that I felt better. We ceremoniously buried the two pieces in the garden that evening.

It really does work, just look at most of the sporting personalities and celebrities, they followed a form of visualisation before they achieved their dream, constantly telling themselves they would reach their goals, imagining the outcome every day and feeling the experience of success as if it was real and tangible.

I also use visualisation to raise my positive vibrations. At the weekends I treat myself to long showers with my favourite piece of music playing on my laptop. I turn it up full blast, get soaked, close my eyes and look towards the spotlight above me. I imagine the light filling my body with clean positive energy, removing all the negativity I have absorbed from stress and other people over the week. It's a great uplifting feeling that really does the trick.

Take the time to chill and zone out, it's a fantastic key to help unlock your inner happiness and spirituality. It keeps you sane and centered in all situations, building an unshakeable reserve of calmness, and a loving nature. No external influences will be able to affect the person who is in touch with their mind and its workings. Imagine a life with no stress, no worries, and no cares. Remember, **"You only have negative experiences because you see them that way"**. One person may perceive missing their train as the most annoying thing in the world, another person may perceive it to be part of life, another may see it is a sign.

If you can control your mind, let it relax and become more aware of the many thoughts that pass through it, you will change your perception for the better. You will also find that your new peace of mind attracts just the right people and circumstances to you. If **The Lost Keys** are keys to open the door to happiness, then controlling the mind is the **master** key. If you can control your mind, you will have found happiness and all the other keys only enhance that happiness. So just chill out, relax and it is yours for the taking!!

7

SOS – Saving Our Planet

♪ *EARTH SONG, MICHAEL JACKSON* ♪

IF OUR PLANET COULD SPEAK I think it would be sending out an SOS, screaming for us to notice the damage we have caused over the last few centuries, and it would be begging us stop the devastation. Since the Iron Age and Industrial Revolution we have sacrificed our natural resources so we could evolve and create the technological advances that now surround us. No one thought about the consequences of mining or burning fossil fuels. Instead of working in harmony with our environment, our scientists and inventors took the easy option of using what was on our doorstep, or beneath it to be more precise. Virtually all of the advances we have created have taken their toll on our environment in some shape or form. Those decisions are in the past, and we can't change them, our present situation however, is something we can all change.

I have a feeling that we are destined for a **360-degree turn around,** reverting back to simpler times in history. Take global warming – all of the processes that burn fossil fuels like cars, planes, and factories destroy environments, destroy the ozone layer, raise sea levels, wipe out species of animals, affect our health, and wreak havoc with the eco-systems. These issues created out of the need for "progress" quite simply destroy **our** planet. Almost every advancement we have engineered has a negative side effect, it's as if we are being punished by the Universe for going against the laws of nature. If you relate my theory to what you currently see in the news, or what you hear on a day-to-day basis, you will know what I am talking about. I have kept a book of newspaper clippings for a few years now, and it shows this turn around quite clearly. Environmental issues are now raised more frequently and in a way that brings awareness to the individual rather than just describing them as a global problem. We are destroying nature for our own "advancement" without putting anything back, which is not a balanced approach. I have already written about the importance of balance in every aspect of life so I will not do so again, but – balance, balance, balance!

I am aware of the science and reasons why Earthquakes and Volcanic Eruptions occur, but on a deeper level I think it could be the Universe or Earths way of subtly telling us to stop destroying the natural resources we have been gifted with. It's not hard to hear the SOS It's about time we took stock of our selfish actions. As I watch the news and read the newspapers I can gradually see that scientists and nations are taking the effects seriously. I hear about carbon emissions all the time, and I hear how people are now encouraged to find alternative means of travel if possible. Carbon offsetting is also constantly in the media and energy saving methods of all kinds promoted in various ways. I just paid £5 to offset the carbon for my skiing trip by ticking an extra box before the payment screen, such a reasonable price for peace of mind don't you think?

After achieving huge feats in the engineering and technological sectors we have finally begun to realise that by creating these advancements we are left with a negative by-product or reaction. The laws of cause and effect are at play once again! The Government, through scientific advisors and research, are finally taking steps to stop or limit the abuse of our planet.

This turn around has indeed begun, but the results will not be seen overnight. I can see it more and more in daily life. For example we are asked to turn off lights when not in use and to recycle. Aerosols have also been modified to protect the ozone layer, carbon offsetting has been employed to deal with the effects of burnt fossil fuels. While both consumption of organic food (which I think will eventually lead to more people growing their own food to ensure natural produce) and the use of re-usable bags instead of plastic bags, have increased. These are all perfect examples of this

simplifying cultural change I am predicting. I am no Nostradamus, but I see this change as a natural progression for our species, or I fear we won't be around much longer! The steps we have taken so far make me feel proud and grateful that we are finally doing things to change our destructive habits.

From a personal perspective, I hold my hand up and admit that my mind slips sometimes. I went to the toilet at work recently and the light was off which made me think the bulb had blown. I then realised someone had made the conscious decision to turn it off. Having given this some thought I realised how crazy it was to leave a light on when no one was in there anyway!! Who would benefit from it being on, the bloody toilet!?

We are all guilty of taking these amenities for granted, we have become dependent on them, and we have become selfish and mindless about the way in which we use them. It is time to wake up to the reality of the huge problems **we** have **all** created. By altering our lazy mindsets on this hugely important issue, and through tiny acts like the one I came across in the toilet at work, and by spreading the word, we really can make a difference.

If one person makes a change for the better, that is a single measure of improvement. It has to start with individuals. Recently I saw a global campaign to turn off all appliances for an hour, (I think it was called Earth Hour) and most people, in most countries around the globe turned off their appliances in a bid to give our planet a break for an hour. It also showed me what can be achieved when people join together to make a positive change. This begins with the individual and grows to a family unit, a village, a city, a country, and eventually leads to the whole world taking action. You, each and every one of you, are as important as a whole nation when it comes to actual action.

The planet is part of each of us. We all have a limited time on it so we should make it as special as possible. Instead of looking at others to make changes to improve our lives, instead of thinking that it doesn't matter, that in my lifetime it will never happen, that it will be alright, and instead of not thinking at all, ***we all need to start acknowledging that our actions contribute to a much bigger picture****. It takes* ***one*** *single person to make a change. Even if you help your fellow human beings by turning off a light, or help by not taking a plastic bag from a supermarket to carry a few cans of Baked Beans, or help by just simply walking more, you will be contributing to the health, harmony, and balance of our home; the EARTH. Just think about what you are doing when you go about your daily life, and the effect you have on our home; that's really all it takes.*

In the future I think we will spend more time on personal development and Spiritual improvement, and less time earning money to support ourselves. But for now – until a larger percentage of the population become more aware of the importance of New Age principles – we will have to balance the two as best we can. It will involve a dramatic shift in our normal ways of thinking, but I can see we will gradually start to look out for each other more, regardless of any possible materialistic gains. We will want to help each other, move forward as a whole, and not just for individual gain.

I am fairly certain that this will happen in a time of great crisis or at a tipping point of emotional despair amongst the masses. In the past, World Wars had the effect of bringing whole nations together to help each other, because it united them in their common goal of survival and preservation. Global warming could be the chance at a United World, united by a drive to survive as a human race, as one whole.

This should hopefully lead to a more balanced social spectrum where the haves and have-nots are no longer so widely separated by economic divides, and where third world countries are no longer indebted to first world countries. The primitive generations of our world managed to exist by exchanging goods and services without the need for complicated economic structures, and I am certain we won't eventually need them in the future. Just take a look at the current economic situation the planet is confronted with at the moment, with credit crunches and recessions looming at every corner; a perfect example that we need to simplify. Once the planet raises it spiritual awareness to a certain level, we will realise that the way forward is to revert back to simpler times in history, whilst keeping the benefits of the automated equipment that frees up our time and makes life easier for us.

I love a good 'end of the world movie', and they always make me shed a tear or two. I think they touch me on a deeper level because these movies involve all of mankind, and the impending doom of the world being destroyed gives them one common purpose – to survive. Given the current state of the world, I think we could all do with a common purpose to unite us. We ALL need to protect the precious limited resource of Mother Earth. We need to get along regardless of religion, race, gender or any other differences. The world has shrunk thanks to modern technological advances, the population is larger, and resources scarcer. We need to be more tolerant of each other and aware of our actions. Start doing your bit to help, the Earth's SOS needs to be heard.

8
Part 1

What You Give Out You Get Back – Karma

♫ *You Get What You Give, New Radicals* ♫

KARMA, LIKE MEDITATION, WAS ONCE a mystical eastern concept lost on most of the western world. It is now slowly creeping into our daily lives in many forms. Over the years I have heard more people drop the phrase "I'll get my Karma for saying that" or "what goes around comes around"

I think we all know that if we do something wrong we will receive a punishment in return. That could be from the State for breaking a law or retaliation from an individual. Karma works in much the same way, but its purpose is to teach us lessons to make us more pure and in touch with the Universe and spirituality. I think that the Ten Commandments in the Bible were a take on the Karmic principles discovered during the age of the Buddha.

Karma is a big part of all of our lives and I want to explain this principle further so we can really appreciate the importance of it. A basic and obvious example that highlights the outcomes of Karmic law would be – If you imagine a person called Matt, who has grown up in a rough neighbourhood with continuous amounts of abuse and lack of love from his parents, he grows up and starts regularly using drugs and alcohol as a way of altering his state of mind to escape the troubles and traumas of his childhood.

He hangs around with a crowd who have similar problems and as they are all in the same situation, they start to rationalise their actions and believe that what they are doing is perfectly normal and acceptable. The group Matt is involved with gets aggressive and abusive due to their constant roller coaster of emotions and lack of self-confidence and identity. Matt uses violence and intimidation tactics to fill his personal void. Our Matt becomes more and more addicted to drugs and feeds his habit by stealing. Little old Matt ends up stealing from his own mother to feed his habit. He gets away with it for a long time but it finally catches up with him! All of those highs and occasional great times begin to crumble around him. His Karma begins to haunt him and comes back to bite him on the arse. He begins to feel a sense of guilt and questions his actions, he eventually gets arrested and sentenced to jail. Matt's kind of lifestyle only stimulates an opposite reaction. A reaction that BALANCES all of the wrong with the right!

The laws of this world that are written down by Government are abided by; for example, you wouldn't down a bottle of Vodka and then hijack a police car, or you wouldn't dream of stealing as many clothes as your baggy jumper would accommodate (and if, like me, you have broken a few laws in your time, you know deep down that it's wrong). So why break the laws of the natural world? **The law of cause and affect**. These were written at the time of the first sparks of the creation of our Universe.

Anyway, now compare Matt's life to that of lets say 'Paul's'. Imagine, Paul lives a simple but happy life, he sees his family regularly and volunteers at a homeless centre every Sunday feeding and talking to people who are normally ignored by the rest of society. Paul enjoys the fresh air and regularly enjoys a run or stroll in the local park, soaking up the beauty of the natural world he is surrounded by. Paul takes time to help people and has compassion for everything and everyone on this planet. He takes time to get to know who he is, and works on self-improvement by looking inwardly and evaluating. He meditates regularly, practices Yoga, and has an unshakable state of mind.

Ask yourself this… if you lived a life like Matt, what do you think your penance would be? What will be the outcome of years of going against the grain? Do you think our Matt will have a life of bliss? Maybe a life of happiness? Or, even a life of eternal joy? Paul, on the other-hand, will be more likely to achieve the things in life that he deserves, his Karmic reward will be equal if not greater than the effort he puts in. The right circumstances and people will be drawn to him in abundance, and unhappiness will rarely knock at his door.

As the laws in society should be followed, so should the Laws of Karma. If not, one way or another you will face an equal reaction to your wrong doings. Our fictitious Matt will be certain to encounter consequences associated with the kind of run-away lifestyle he led.

I had a friend that always managed to get phones "off the back of a lorry" and usually within a month or two she would lose or have the phone stolen along with something else like a purse or her handbag. I could clearly see it was Karma working its little magic!!

I have realised that the more spiritual I become, the faster Karma returns to me, and speaking to a person in a New Age book shop recently, he confirmed my belief, and said it was another unwritten law of the Universe. How many more are there I thought?! The more aware you are, the faster your Karma returns to you, both negative and positive. This quickly helps you to become a better person.

I see the laws of cause and effect in motion and can't help but ponder on every thought or action and its possible consequences – it drove me mad for a while, but now it is part of my life. If I find myself laughing at someone who has tripped over in front of me, I immediately find myself walking into a lamppost or falling flat on my face! You soon learn to stop laughing at others misfortunes when you're faced with those instant consequences. Thom and Helen my best mates are very aware of my instant boomeranging Karma and it is now a running joke. The more spiritually connected I become, the more I am made to take responsibility for my actions, so the old adage of "with great power, comes great responsibility" is never truer than when you find yourself on the spiritual path.

On a related note, I have to mention reincarnation here. This is a subject that has only entered my world a year prior to The Lost Keys going to print. It is a deep subject with many diversions, but I am going to paraphrase my understanding of it as it answers some profound questions that we all share.

Throughout my spiritual development I have always had difficulty understanding why some people are born disabled or handicapped. I could not find a justifiable reason, or logic to it. I had a suspicion that it was to teach them or their families various lessons, like patience or having to rely on others for help. When I learnt about the theories of reincarnation I realised I had hit the nail on the head. Learning about reincarnation was another marvellous synchronicity event in itself, which you will find occurs more and more frequently as you unlock The Lost Keys. After watching a blind man board the train at Waterloo I stared out the window and into nowhere, asking why I was so lucky to have been blessed with a fully working body. That very evening I finished the current book I was reading and plucked another at random from my well-stocked cupboard (mostly hand-me-downs from my Mums collection). I realised I was now being taught the principles of reincarnation in a book that I would never have dreamt would contain such information from its title alone. As gob-smacked as I was at yet another great example of the ways the world can work for you, I read on, and absorbed the ancient theories of reincarnation.

Before this discovery my Mum's friends openly talked about their past lives, and I secretly thought they had lost the plot. Mum personally claims to have lived during the age of Atlantis, as a Witch in the Dark Ages, and during the French Revolution among many others. I thought it meant physically in the same body. Rather confusing really. But after picking my jaw up from the floor after reading that random book I learnt that it is our spirit, that guiding thing above the mind that does the reincarnation bit. The Spirit is an essence, a living energy that never dies and is the real "us" – a guiding hand that contains our purpose. It is temporarily linked to this thing we call our body.

The Spirit has been around since the creation of time, it moves through time as if time had no meaning. It is infinite. It leaves a body when it is time, when that person dies. It then finds a new host in a chosen time period. Each time taking with it the lessons learnt from the previous life. The Spirit gradually becomes a storehouse of valuable information. When things are familiar when they have no reason to be, or when you feel like you already know a person but have never previously met them; it is because you have interacted with them in a previous existence. If, in a previous lifetime you had done something bad to someone and had not worked out the

Karma, you would have the chance to do so in another lifetime. You might come across that Spirit in this life, and have to work it out now.

I wondered if Mum had abused my Dad in a previous life and him 'returning the favour' to her in this lifetime was her Karma coming back to her, if not slightly delayed. She knowingly smiled, didn't bat an eyelid and totally agreed, saying that I had clearly mastered the principles of reincarnation! Turns out she had pondered the very same thing not so long ago!

The Spirit also doesn't discriminate between male and female, all of us have most certainly been both in past lives. It's a great way to find the balance between yin and yang, masculine and feminine. The Spirit carries on leap-froging from host to host, working out Karma, learning everything necessary to finally leave the cycle of reincarnation to achieve enlightenment. Where that leads I have no idea, I haven't got that far yet, no doubt a book or person will teach me that when I am ready!

If this all seems far fetched and mumbo jumbo fair play. I wouldn't have tolerated this at the beginning of my quest, and probably even three years ago for that matter. But ask yourself this, do you ever find yourself fascinated or intrigued by something that you would otherwise have no reason to be interested in? It might not yet be apparent, but it will show up in the strangest of places. It is usually about a period of time in history or a random subject. I found myself fascinated with The Knights Templar and Crusades after reading just one single sentence about them in a book. It sparked off a huge thirst for more information including movies, books, and music all resulting in a feeling of familiarity. Also Egyptians, and Carl Jung (who by the way is someone I totally relate too, even though he has long since snuffed it) found their way into my life. I am now of the firm belief that these were part of, or some of my past lives.

Have a rummage around your psyche and you will find it truly intriguing. You can also visit mediums to recall past lives, it's slightly like hypnosis as they place you in a trance so you can more easily delve into your Spirit and recall your Spirit's past. It could be a great way to understand yourself more.

A lot of issues people have that are not attributable to early childhood, are a result of negative things that happened in a past life. It is your Spirit's way of telling you to work out these issues carried over from another life. Live a good honest life and Karma will be kind to you, the more spiritual you become the faster you will see its effect. Remember that you need certain lessons to grow, so even a saint will be sent tests that might not actually be related to Karma. Ultimately; what you give out, you get back.

8
Part 2

Compassion vs Terrorism – Karma

♪ *WHERE IS THE LOVE, BLACK EYED PEAS* ♪

KARMA AND COMPASSION GO HAND-IN-HAND. Acts of compassion and empathy are great ways of creating positive Karma. Worryingly, and rather depressingly there are those that have no sense of visible compassion or empathy. These sorts of people range from racists, to religious extremists, to homophobics, to bullies. All of them, from the school-ground bully to a member of Al-Qaeda have the same thing in common; a lack of empathy and compassion for the people they verbally or physically abuse. I think that these sorts of behaviours can only be a result of one, or all of these four things:

1. A lack, or misinterpretation of education and knowledge.

2. An abusive or troubled background that has not been dealt with on a mental and spiritual level.

3. A feeling of not belonging to society.

4. Fear of the person, group, religion, theory, or organisation they are targeting.

None of the points above are beyond rectifying, but none of the points above can **ever** be rationalised. I simply cannot understand the need to dislike someone to the extent of causing physical harm or verbal abuse, causing the attacked to feel smaller than the attacker. That's what it boils down to, being attacked. Perhaps I feel so strongly about it because I have seen this first hand with my Mum and Dad, but I am not just talking about a few punches and kicks to someone you have had an argument or disagreement with, this goes much deeper than that.

Let's take religious extremists and the whole terrorism issue as an example. In particular take suicide bombers claiming to be martyrs who believe that their sacrifice is for 'the greater good' of their religion and they will be rewarded in Paradise (Islam's version of Heaven) for their efforts. When I worked in Iraq back in 2005 the main cause of violence and death was attributed to Sectarian violence. This involved fighting between the Sunni Muslim tribes and the Shia Muslims. On countless occasions they would attack each other's mosques in

Basra killing hundreds of innocent people in a blood bath under the pretence of "religion".

I could almost understand when they attacked British and coalition forces, *almost*. They attacked the British as the uneducated or misinformed Iraqi extremists were of the impression that we had taken over the Country unlawfully and for our own benefits (oil apparently!), so it was their way of retaliating – I found this easier to understand than their sectarian violence. I couldn't begin to imagine how they could kill each other in a time when I thought they should be working together to help rebuild their country after the rule of Saddam Hussein. I strongly believe that this shocking lack of compassion and empathy is down to my first point – a lack, or misinterpretation of education and knowledge.

Just on the oil issue, one thing I will say is that we, the UK, never went to war in Iraq for oil. I don't know where that came from, but from all the intelligence I have seen over the years I can put my neck on the line and say I have never even seen a mention of that theory which was fanned by the media.

As I have previously said, I do not profess to be an expert on religion, but from what I have read about each major religious sect, none condone murder of any kind, let alone the murder and slaughter of their fellow 'brothers'. All, if not most, somehow teach the idea of turning the other cheek. Religions generally **do not** condone the act of violence in the face of violence. This concept might seem very alien to most people new to any type of religious or spiritual belief, and actually performing this idea may be easier said than done.

As for religious extremism I think the main problem is down to the changes these religions have undergone throughout the centuries. It seems to me that the very foundations of religion have been shaken to the core as a result of the changes in the world today. In such a relatively short period of time we have, as a race, evolved **so very** rapidly. What used to take months and years to get messages to places like the Middle East now takes seconds thanks to the Internet and TV. Stories and facts about religions and behaviours of people in the West have reached the Middle East (the most obvious and largest example of religious extremism). This has raised questions and doubts about the strict laws and teachings they have received through the ages unchallenged, unrivalled, and unquestioned. Now that these populations have more comparisons available to their once insular and isolated countries they can put their religion into context with the rest of the world. The same goes for Muslims raised in Western Countries who are confronted with the duality of living in the Western World while trying to find an identity through their religion.

I think that this has raised questions as to what their religion stands for in this modern age. By questioning a religion that has been around since the dawn of time, and a religion that literally governs the daily life of millions of people, uncertainty and irrational behaviour arises. This makes way for new ideology, and becomes easier for extremists to preach new, or to change the meaning of, certain teachings under the facade of restoring the faith. While at the same time giving themselves the power they so desperately crave.

The extremists and terrorists have taken advantage of the uncertainty that the various followers are experiencing, seemingly giving the followers the answers they require to cure doubts that have arisen from our new age of modern advancement and thinking. Simply put, they are offering a form of identity, in a time of need.

The followers are desperately searching for a way of holding onto their beliefs, whilst at the same time trying to make sense of the changes and new information they have about other religions, other behaviours, other customs, as well as all the new scientific information available to them that also contradicts a vast amount of their ancient religious laws and beliefs. This is why so many have misinterpreted, or have a lack of understanding of their own belief systems and follow these outrageous claims in the name of "religion". In this desperate search they think they have found a purpose to life, and this is what their underlying drive is – **a sense of purpose**.

Given time I hope that these followers begin to realise this, and see their religious truths for what they are, and not what a few twisted and warped individuals have turned them into.

In 2010 President Obama said in his speech to mark the anniversary of the 9/11 attacks in America – *"It was not a religion that attacked us on that September day, it was Al Qaeda, a sorry band of men that perverts religion".* I thought this was a perfect summary of terrorism.

That day shook the world. I was bunking off school at the time and remember every channel suddenly switching to an image of a building I had never heard of, and then, as I was watching it live, another plane crashed into the side of the Twin Towers. I am sure by now it won't surprise you to learn that I found myself in tears as that fateful day unfolded. Nat, a friend from school, came over in the afternoon and we both just sat there gobsmacked at what we were witnessing. I think we will all remember where we were when we heard the news. What Obama was getting across was that Muslims weren't the enemy, it was a few men who happened to call themselves Muslims.

I strongly believe the extremism element has developed from a group, or perhaps even a single individual, preaching the idea that martyrdom is acceptable in any given circumstance. Their bottom line is that Allah permits the killing of fellow human beings if it causes justice and sustains the Islamic traditions. Some Islamic teachings also guarantee entry to Paradise if the Martyr dies in his mission. But I ask you, what God could ever permit such an atrocity on humankind? – To take another persons free will to live? None in my eyes, and I am sure most of the mainstream Imams would agree with me too.

This is such a complex issue that couldn't possibly be solved overnight, and the Middle East peace process will take time and flexibility by all those countries involved, and more importantly the people involved. I imagine that the religions that harbour extremism will adapt and change over the years to incorporate and include the new world truths and discoveries. The truth will eventually dawn on the misguided few.

Nobody wants war and death anymore, its so passé. Having visited the most hostile countries in the world including Iraq and Afghanistan, I can categorically say that they are beautiful countries with so much potential, and the poor civilians are such nice loving people who only want peace. I long for the day we can travel free from fear and visit these places as tourists once again.

"War – What is it good for, absolutely nothing." Or so I thought. I once believed this famous song lyric until I had to reevaluate my morals. During one of my weekend shifts where I had to sleep over in Downing Street for the entire weekend, we received reports that Gaddafi was using his military to fire on civilians and discussions were taking place about military action.

I was very withdrawn during this period; I knew what was at stake. I kept thinking, "Oh God, not another Iraq/ Afghanistan." When the decision was taken on military action my heart sank.

I voiced my concerns to a senior official (now a friend) involved in the process, and he assured me it would not be another Iraq and that casualties would be minimal as we would have no "feet on ground" (soldiers in Libya basically).

I hoped he was right, and felt in one day that my morals had changed. War should be an absolute last resort, and it should justify the means. In this instance France and the UK helped to secure Gaddafi's downfall and saved civilian lives. The ends seemed to have justified the means. I felt bad and in some ways guilty to have been present during this period, and as I tucked myself into the uncomfortable single bed next door to the PM's flat, I drifted off thinking about our planes on their way to Libya.

The next thing I knew I was abruptly woken by 'The Red Phone' and noticed the time read 04:00. The bubbly but slightly tired lady on Switchboard informed me the Prime Minister was on the line - it was time to update him, so I checked the details with the Ministry of Defence and reported back.

The mission was successful and many more followed before Gaddafi was found in a drain, quite poetic really given that he called the rebels "rats" in one of his speeches! This entire experience was a big lesson for me about compassion, and that sometimes you have to do what appears to be wrong, in order to do the right thing.

For me, the hardest thing about having compassion for others is that I know we can play a part in others suffering, directly or indirectly. War is one example of indirect involvement, we just have to hope that any future wars are absolutely necessary and happen for the right reasons.

The most important thing for all religions and people to remember is that we are all here at the same time on this planet, all here together and for a purpose. We breathe the same air and are born equal. We need to get along in harmony with each other and stop killing our fellow man in the name of religion or justice. Jews, Hindus, Christians, Muslims, Buddhists, and Spiritualists have no reason to try and out-do each other or make each other convert.

We are all searching for the one thing that binds us together, which is our quest for happiness, by whichever method or religion we decide to choose. As the Dali Lama says "Everyone wants to be happy and not to suffer".

9

Rabbit Food –
Diet & Killing of Animals

♪ *Circle Of Life, Elton John* ♪

THE PREVIOUS LOST KEY ON Karma and compassion leads nicely onto the negative effects of killing animals and eating meat. I have to be careful with what I am about to write, as I don't want to come across as a hardcore animal rights fanatic. I am not, and I am not writing this to convert you all too eating rabbit food. This Lost Key is not just about being a vegetarian, it will also help you think about what you are putting into your body.

Whatever religion or belief system you follow, and

even if you don't have one, the killing of humans is not encouraged in any way. Why is that? Is it because as people we can recognise the importance of another's life? Is it because we are conscious of our own existence? Do we just know that it's morally wrong? I think the answer is yes to all of the above, so why should the same not apply to animals?

There are so many arguments and counter-arguments to vegetarianism so I think the best way forward is to give the arguments here, and offer my perspective.

Many carnivores I know usually start with the:

"It's innate, we were born to eat meat, and our ancestors before us hunted for survival". That is true – caveman hunted animals to survive, and I suppose it is still a natural instinct in all of us. However we have evolved far beyond our primal ancestors, we have ships and planes that import and export all sorts of exotic vegetables, pulses, and grains that were simply not available to the isolated pre-historic civilisations. We have no need to "hunt" for our survival anymore as food comes to us, in some cases right to our door, and we can buy clothes without using animal skins and fur! To put the term "hunt" into context in our modern age I mean go to the supermarket or butchers and buy a slab of flesh. If you're a meat eater imagine having to kill your own chicken, or kill your own calf.

The next, and usually most surprising comment is *"We need meat for protein, and it's the biggest source of it"*. Again, it's true but not without criticism. Due to the advances in our world with travel between continents taking hours not months, all sorts of foods have become available to us such as; lentils, chick peas, kidney beans, mango's, bananas, seaweed, cashew nuts – I could go on and on. As a vegetarian I get all my protein from things like cheese, nuts, and pulses that are more than adequate in replacing the protein contained in meat and fish. You just have to take more of an interest in what you are putting into your body.

Once a carnivore has heard why I have made the decision to become vegetarian they usually ask, *"Do you not get bored? What do you actually eat?"* This is my favourite question because it shows they are interested in vegetarian cooking. The first answer is obviously "No I do not get bored" because I ate more exotic and interesting foods in my first year of being a vegetarian than I have in my whole life! I have also become an excellent cook (even though I do say so myself!) in the process. I only buy fresh foods, and try not to buy anything with excessive additives or colourings. I rarely use recipe books, I see things I like in the supermarket, or things I have never tried and then I let my imagination go wild. Granted sometimes I will never eat it again as it tasted vile (on one occasion I even gagged!), but nine times out of ten it is gorgeous and I have great satisfaction knowing my time and effort went into something that fuels my mind, body and Spirit. I also never overbuy and never throw anything away as I am aware that people in the world are starving every minute, so I force myself to be extra creative at the end of each shopping week with whatever is left over. I suppose it is like rationing during the war, using everything in your cupboard to avoid waste. Sometimes it is a challenge, but gets those creative juices flowing. Ultimately my diet can't be as boring and as unimaginative as the old meat and two vege dishes I used to polish off.

The other point sometimes raised is the fact that most animals are bred for slaughtering, and the meat eaters in some bizarre way find that more acceptable. Fundamentally the animal is still dying no matter what reasoning you give to try and rationalise it. In some countries, only when an animal dies naturally is it used for food, which in my eyes is a far more natural way of doing things.

Once friends and others have asked all of the above they begin to respect my decisions, but will usually say, "I couldn't do it, I like the taste of meat too much"

Animals move and are aware of their surroundings, feel pain and fear, and on that basic level they are the same as us. Most sane people would not kill another human being by choice. Why then, are so many people happy to gorge on the flesh of a dead animal? I think the main reason is because you can't see how it is slaughtered. You don't hear the screams, or the squeals of pain and agony, nor do you see the blood stained instruments that are used everyday on millions of creatures that we share this planet with.

I became a vegetarian when I was about ten years old after I saw my Mum watching a programme about how they slaughtered animals for the production of food. She wasn't aware that I was standing behind the sofa watching it. I cried my eyes out all night and said I didn't want to eat meat ever again. Time passed and I went back to eating chicken but stayed off red meat altogether.

Eventually, at sixteen, I went back to eating all types of meat as I was worried I was too skinny for my age, and I think I just lost sight of that very thought provoking programme I had seen when I was so young.

Once I found spirituality and began to understand more about the world we inhabit, I decided to become a vegetarian. This meant I was not going to eat meat *or fish*. Some vegetarians don't eat meat but still eat fish; which is technically called a Pescatarian. Granted this is a **fantastic** start, and being a Pescatarian is a far more spiritual way of living in harmony with nature than that of a carnivore and should be commended. Anyway, after making this decision not to eat meat or fish I realised it was a very poorly timed decision because I was just about to depart to work in Iraq. This posting to Iraq was to last for a minimum of six months, and a maximum of a year. I was briefed about the lifestyle I was to expect about two months before leaving the UK. I was told I was going to live in a compound that I couldn't leave during my time there, the catering would be provided, and as we couldn't take a trip to the local supermarket (for obvious reasons) we basically ate what we were given. And as everything had to come from Kuwait by road, we were given very basic rations with vegetarian options few and far between. I vowed that as soon as my posting was finished I would become 100% vegetarian.

It's been well over seven years now since I left Basra and became vegetarian and I genuinely, hand on heart, don't miss any meat or fish. I feel healthier, happier, more energetic, and I have this strange feeling of being lighter!

It does make me fart more but hey, that's a small price to pay!

Without wanting to sound condescending or patronising I feel that meat eaters can be ignorant, naïve, and selfish. I doubt that many carnivores would eat meat if they had to butcher it themselves! Imagine this really carefully – would you go out into your back garden, look one of your lambs in the eye, watch it graze, watch it breathing the same air as you, listen to it go "baargh", and then load your shot gun and blast a bullet between its eyes and through its head? Would you then rip off the wool, hack off the head with a hacksaw then let all the blood that was once pumping oxygen around its body drain out? Would you then take a knife and start hacking bits of flesh off its carcass to store for your lamb chops, or mince for spaghetti bolognaise? If you're honest with yourself I bet you would rather go without. Just because this process is removed from your vision doesn't mean it goes away, it really doesn't, it is happening every minute, everyday. It's very naïve to think otherwise. Animals are being cruelly slaughtered like this all the time because of the demand for meat.

When demand lessens, so will the supply! It's really that simple. The same goes for fish, even though they are not butchered in the same way, it would be the same equivalent as humans being submerged under water until we could no longer breath. It sounds like a horrific nightmare to me. Until recently I thought fish didn't make any noise when they died. But I saw a clip on the news about tuna fishing in the Mediterranean and as these massive fish were lying on the shore of the sea, trapped in a net, wriggling and gasping for their last breath a fisherman stabbed a metal rod into its head and I heard a sound much like a scream. I cried at the sight of it, the water lapping up the beach was saturated dark red with **blood**. This was a real eye-opener.

I have three goldfish – Eddie, Patsie, and Bubbles, and everyone that has seen them have said how clever they are. They follow you when you walk past them and they always know which end to swim to when its food time. Even fish, it appears, are self-aware!

Most people enjoy the ease of popping down the butchers and ordering meat from a chicken, a cow, or a pig, just because they like the taste and it gives them protein!! In order to change this type of mindset all it takes is a little bit of thought for these creatures that are so aware of their surroundings.

So far I have only discussed the bad karmic effects of killing animals for food as my reason for becoming a vegetarian, but it's not the only reason. There are so many more that may give you a different perspective.

1. Another reason I decided to become vegetarian was because I went on holiday to Ibiza some years back and one morning after a particularly heavy night out, my friends and I all went for breakfast at a local café. They ordered fry-ups but I couldn't stomach it so I ordered yogurt with fruit and honey. As all of our 'hangover cures' appeared from the kitchen and were placed in front of us I realised my hangover cure was still fresh, colourful, and alive almost, whereas looking at my friends plates all I could see was

brown, grease, and dead animals. Mine looked more appealing and vibrant, and trusting my sense of sight I decided to try and eat appealing, alive looking foods from then on. I delved further into my mind and wondered what was better for my body, things that are already dead and frozen for days and weeks before ever reaching our plates, or living colourful things like fruit and vegetables containing living energy. The more I thought about it the more it intrigued me, it felt as if I had just had an epiphany and awakened something inside of me that was so obvious I couldn't believe how I had ever managed to overlook it. It is so simple – what you put into your body is reflected in the outputs, including health and positive mindsets.

2. By becoming vegetarian and basing your diet on whole foods (nothing added or taken away) you will inevitably be living a healthier life than that of a meat eater. I mentioned in the Lost Key about drugs that our bodies are natural creations and what we put into them should also be natural. We were not designed to intake chemicals that increase the natural life of food products, nor were we designed to eat colourings and other unnatural additives. Too much animal fat, sugar and salt lead to heart disease and diabetes to name just a few of the western illnesses, caused by unnatural eating habits. Think about the BSE crisis we faced not so long ago, it was because farmers were feeding their livestock unnatural

feed and the result of this was the catastrophic BSE disease. Scrapie in sheep was the same story and Bird Flu yet another example. I bet we will never see a disease associated with natural whole foods.

3. The environment suffers as a direct result of meat farming. A vast majority of the crops in the world are used to feed animals bred for meat and could otherwise be used to feed starving people of third world countries. Cows are bred en masse to meet the demand for beef. These millions of cows give out vast amounts of methane, which is one of the biggest contributing factors to the global warming crisis we are all currently facing. Plus, the cows are taking up precious space that could be used for crop and cereal growth. This was a big headline story during the Copenhagen Climate Summit, and quite a serious cause of concern.

4. Another good reason is that it is simply cheaper to be vegetarian, even if you bought only organic food, it will be cheaper than buying meat. I couldn't believe the price of bacon the other day when I was looking for some cheese (No readers, I wasn't tempted, even though the smell of cooked bacon still stirs something in me!). The spare money you save could be used to experiment with foods you have never tried before to increase your appreciation for the many options now available to us.

5. I remember when I moved to London back in 2003 when I was embarking on so many new things, the one thing I found really easy was cooking. In fact it was so easy thinking of different combinations of meat and two vege that it got boring very quickly. After a while it felt like I *had* to have some kind of version of meat and two vege every day, the only time I ever deviated from that was with fish or pasta – not very adventurous or varied. Vegetarian cooking has brought so much more colour and variety into my diet, with loads of foreign specialities available, it opened my eyes to all the tastes and flavours available in the world. I love Middle Eastern food at the moment, which usually consists of a variety of smaller dishes being eaten at the same time, which is a real treat for all of your senses.

I think I have covered the main reasons I am a vegetarian, but at this point in the book I would like to mention that it's not just the killing of animals for food that I disagree with, but also the senseless killing of animals in the name of sport. By now I hope the idea of Karma has hit home and you can clearly see that there is a cause and effect for everything we do. So it goes without saying that the killing of a living creature on this planet, man or beast, is wrong, and goes against the unwritten rules of society and the Universe.

Anything from fox hunting to something as seemingly insignificant as stamping on a spider or trapping a mouse [No word of a lie, a mouse has just ran past the edge of the sofa and it scared the shit out of me and my heart is going ten to the dozen…but I didn't jump up and try to kill it because once I had rationalised my behaviour and told myself it was no threat, the fright went away. Thinking about it, fields were once their habitat before we humans developed the land. It's not like the little thing is going to drag me off and throw me over the balcony! – Maybe rationalising our fears is a way to change out mindsets]. Anyway, I digress, before I was so rudely interrupted by little 'mousey' I was saying that something so small and seemingly insignificant to us still has an important role on this planet, it fits into the whole grand scheme of things, and is here for a reason, as we are.

If you are still not convinced about the rights of animals then think about a creature as small as the ant. They follow the basic rules we do; they work, they eat, they sleep and they have hierarchical structures. We are bigger, and can talk, but we all breathe the same air and inhabit the same place. It is simply co-existence.

What right does any one of us have to kill animals for food, or to murder them in the name of sport or entertainment? We are not barbarians or primitive animals anymore, it's time our minds caught up with our rapid evolution. If I saw a poor defenceless animal being slaughtered, screaming out in sheer agony as another person butchered it, I would undoubtedly feel compassion for that creature and I am sure you would too – so please give it more thought next time you kill, inadvertently or not, a living creature.

When you next buy or cook meat ask yourself how it got to your plate, and then ask yourself if you're willing to carry on pretending that you don't care? Above all, ask yourself would you personally kill the thing now resting on your plate??

Here is an abstract thought for you; maybe all this war and death we are surrounded by is **Karma's** way of paying us back for the daily murder of millions of animals to satisfy our selfish desire to eat meat.

Something more generally on diet – soft drinks and many squashes contain behaviour-changing chemicals. We saw dramatic behaviour changes (for the better) once Mum put some of the foster children on natural foods and fresh juices. This is exactly the kind of thing Jamie Oliver was campaigning about when he challenged (rightly so) the Government about the quality of school dinners.

In just over ten years I can see that my epiphany on holiday is what the rest of the world is seeing now, and they are not just seeing it, it has been proved beyond reasonable doubt. The most obvious example is the Government's recommendation of eating five pieces of fruit or vegetable a day. It doesn't say eat one item of poultry, two items of livestock and one aquatic animal a day! Organic food is more popular than ever, vegetarianism is on the up (I don't have statistics but I am 100% sure the Vegetarian Society would agree with me on that), there have been more programmes about healthier eating, the majority of people are eating wholemeal or brown bread, 100% natural smoothies have exploded onto the market, and even major fast-food chains have had to change their game-plan by advertising salads to their consumers. To be honest, I think meat will become more of a luxury in the future as populations and costs continue to rise. People will be forced to change their eating habits.

Things are changing, and its bloody brilliant they are changing for the better. It's all happening around us and I can't help but give a little smile when I see the evidence in the media!

If after hearing all of the above you still cannot bring yourself to give up meat, then buy organic produce or cut down a bit. At least with organic food you can buy your flesh knowing the animals had a better life than those squashed up in some tiny barn or field. The same goes for eggs, free range all the way people! That's what its all about, the cleaner and more natural the input, the cleaner and more natural the output!

10

Choose Your Future – The Power to Change

♪ *HALL OF FAME, THE SCRIPT FT WILL.I.AM* ♪

A FEW YEARS BACK, FOLLOWING A busy period travelling overseas with work and looking for a new flat, I eventually moved into a place in Battersea with my friend Jen. It had the most amazing views of London for our budget. Everywhere you looked you could see lights in residential buildings. The views – even though industrial – were awe-inspiring and it once again reaffirmed my connection with something much bigger than just 'me'.

It was an eye-opening realisation to experience that connection simply by looking at a manmade landscape that I once viewed as just a concrete jungle. I described the appreciation of nature in an earlier Lost Key, and I suppose that feeling, as I looked over London, was a similar appreciation because I felt part of the big city that always has so much energy and movement twenty-four hours a day. More than that, I am connected to all of the millions of people that are going about their daily business, and I am sharing the same space and experiences in some way, shape or form.

As I sat on the breakfast bar (sounds posh, but it really wasn't!) and gazed out of the window towards Canary Wharf, I could see row after row of Victorian houses all converted into flats with the occasional high rise building breaking the single level of rooftops. I saw one person watching TV, and directly above that another person was casually reading a book and enjoying a glass of red wine. Those people were living their lives as they wanted to, given the natural confines of their environment and situation. What I find striking when contemplating the variety of all these lifestyles is the enormous differences in the lives of individuals. What is even more interesting is that this occurs even when these individuals have a similar materialistic level of existence. For example, two people on the same wage in the same area of London will fill each of what I consider "precious days" with completely different activities. I have met people who wake at five in the morning and go jogging to welcome in their day. They might spend most of their lunch running or getting out of the office to free their mind from work tribulations. Then they go home, eat a freshly cooked meal and study for an Open University course or attend language lessons. On the other hand I have met people who are late into work, eat at their desk and go home to cook a frozen meal from the supermarket and watch TV all evening until its time for 'Bedfordshire'.

I am not saying that either existence is right or wrong, but it's amazing to think of the vast difference in lifestyles between two people. What an individual is capable of is a result of their **attitude, thinking, and motivation**. Without these three things I don't think a lot can happen, granted material wealth can help, but fundamentally we need to have the right mindset and motivation to get something out of life. There is nothing more annoying than hearing someone moan about something in their life that they are capable of changing. If you want it, then just bloody do it, stop moaning about it and **take action**. Einstein once said, "Insanity is doing the same thing, over and over again, and expecting different results". Ain't that the truth! The more you push yourself the more you will learn and develop as a person. There are limits, but you will only know how far you can go once you make that first leap into the unknown.

We all know how easy it is to settle for what we have and avoid change, but like water left too long we can grow stagnant. If we stop seeking improvement then we are saying to ourselves (and the world) that we have no need to improve – remember this when you become complacent – this thought gives me the extra motivation I need to move forward. I have a list hidden away of everything I want to do in my life, from things like visiting all Seven Wonders of the World, to learning the piano, and I am determined to tick everything off on that ever-growing list!

Change keeps life interesting, it shakes things up and has the ability to teach us so many things. I have uprooted my life on several occasions; moved country and arrived at destinations barely knowing myself let alone my surroundings and other people. The same goes for travelling by myself, or as Wesley my friend once aptly said, "travelling *with* myself". I find that when you are removed from the familiar surroundings of your home country, and especially when you are alone, you find yourself relying more on your instincts, intuition and gut feelings. You notice more things, you feel the vibes of crowds, you are more aware as if your Spirit is guiding you to keep you safe and on the search for new insights. All we need is a small amount of faith that it will be a beneficial and positive change, and that's what it will become.

It amazes me when people tell me they don't have a dream. Hope and dreaming are wonderful things, and a great way to start achieving what is important to us. Now more than ever, people are following their dreams, their destiny, their calling, whatever you want to call it. It is an exciting time, and if you are being true to yourself, then you will succeed in achieving your dreams. Dare to dream. Reach for the stars, push yourself, we are capable of so much. Imagine if the great people of our history had not followed their dreams. Imagine if Thomas Edison hadn't followed his dream of creating a light bulb, or Alexander Graham Bell hadn't invented the telephone.

We blame the lack of time for not being able to do

what we want, or what we need to do. We use time as an excuse not to do things, and by saying we don't have time or are too old I think we are just settling for second best. **Find the time, before you end up on your deathbed, thinking about the many things you didn't do.** My Mum is actually a prime example of a person who curses time; she has a very busy life running around like a headless chicken (as she puts it!). Her day usually consists of all sorts of people dropping in unexpectedly, looking after the kids that she fosters, shopping for her friends who don't have cars, and she also has a menagerie of animals to contend with– at the moment she has 5 dogs, 12 puppies, 2 cats, 5 kittens, 1 wild cat, 2 gerbils, and a partridge in a pear tree (slight exaggeration with the bird). With all of these commitments she constantly says she runs out of time.

I suggested to her that she should try and organise her days like a General in the army to give her more structure and rigidity, but I think she likes flitting from one thing to the next and her life doesn't really allow for more structure. If for example she got up two hours earlier every day and didn't answer the phone she would have an extra 56 hours a month. You could argue that she would be more tired, but within reason tiredness is just a state of mind. Your body obviously needs rest but you probably don't need as much as you think. Once you are up and doing things it soon wears off. Take the example I gave of the early morning jogger, and I actually know loads of people like that – if they can fit all of those activities and self-improvement into their days, then all of us should be able to because we are all essentially the same. Don't be using time as an easy excuse to put off the things you want or should do. Regrets are things none of us should ever experience, and this thought is something I have kept repeating to myself since I was about thirteen. **"I will not have any regrets"**.

Choose your future, take responsibility for your life. Your **attitude, thinking, and motivation** are the only things that stand in your way, and I think we all know that. Don't give up on your dream and settle for the easy life. When you decide that your dream is no longer worth the hassle or the energy then you stop living life properly. Keep dreaming, changing direction, pushing yourself, improving yourself and living with enthusiasm. I know it is really hard, I know it is difficult and painful, but when you find yourself in a black hole, either materially or spiritually say "**NO**" and don't accept it. Why the hell should you let yourself get into that situation?

A dear friend of mine is currently jobless and has been for several months. He has so much potential, a fantastic personality, and a kind heart. He does not deserve to be in this situation. These moments in life are consuming – you get drawn into the negatives and forget the positives aspects of your life. Giving up and accepting your situation is always the easier option. I know in the current climate of financial instability there will be many people in similar situations. The key is to rise above it, **fight**, and fight with everything you have to stay afloat. You have no reason to accept unfavourable conditions, you have potential and a purpose to fulfil, so fight for it. However, there are still lessons to be learnt from these painful and hard moments in life. It just so happens that this period in my friend's life has given him time to reflect on his inner world, his inner psyche, and I think this will be his chance to find Spirituality and the true meaning of life. **A gift wrapped in rather ugly wrapping paper I guess.**

Lessons are everywhere, as I have already outlined in The Lost Key "Setbacks & Experiences" – but this doesn't mean sitting back and accepting the shit life has to throw at you. It means learning the lessons the Universe wants us to learn, while fighting to live out our true destiny. Our true destiny is something only we can discover by looking inwardly. These tests will ultimately make us stronger, more rounded, and at the same time more grounded people. It is just another hurdle we must face on the long race, if you fall over on your first attempt then get up and try again, remembering how you got your scars and grazes. **You don't fail until you stop trying.**

I was out with a friend from work a while back, and as we were walking along the High street in East London he said "do you mind if I smoke", with a glint in his eye as if saying "please stop me!" I replied with a smile "no it's your choice, carry on, nothing to do with me". He said "Oh pleeeease tell me not to, as it will give me some extra willpower if I hear it from someone else"

He was slightly joking but nonetheless it was interesting. I gave up smoking because like everything in my life it was all or nothing, I did things to such extremes that it was borderline psychopathic! Anyway, I got sick of smoking forty cigarettes a night at weekends and decided it was not doing me any favours so I stopped cold turkey on New Years Day 2007. I hate the smell of it now and don't want to smoke ever again thanks to a change in thinking, attitude and my motivation to want to stop. I recommended the same approach to my friend if he was serious about giving up, I said the same goes for anything you want to change in life – you need the approval of your mind to actually make it happen. He did eventually stop on his own accord about three years later, and now feels fantastic.

You have to make your own discoveries in life otherwise you will never learn the lessons first hand. That's why I would never wish to change anyone's personality or belief systems. If they are interested in my beliefs then I am happy to share with them, but I would rather they found their own path of self-discovery, that way they can experience the ups and downs for themselves and be proud of any resulting achievements. **<u>True learning, I once heard, comes from actual experience not theory</u>**. To *experience* a teaching or lesson is to fully know it yourself, and not just the idea behind it. This very book is about my life and experiences, I hope it will help others, but I do not wish anyone to blindly accept my advice or the lessons I am sharing. You will know what works for you, and what feels right.

Having started my Spiritual quest when I was nineteen, I have followed a random trail and along the way craved information on certain subjects that led me onto other ones. It soon snowballed out of control and now the Universe provides me with exactly what I am looking for, at exactly the right moment in my life. I was following a path of my choice, a path that was unclear at the start but felt so natural to follow. I learnt about things that interested me deeply, and at a time that was right for me. Had I learnt about reincarnation at the start of my quest, I could have shrugged the whole New Age thing off as a load of mumbo jumbo.

Our journeys, our quests, our paths, are totally individual. What is right for some is wrong for others, so follow your intuition, that guiding hand that we all know is there. Have faith and follow the path that is right for you. Choose how you want to live your life, what you want from it, and go out and find it. Have the **motivation** to achieve your desires and you will.

We all have an internal body clock that tells us when we are ready for certain discoveries. My own spiritual alarm clock went off relatively early, my Mum's when she was middle aged, and others sometimes never hear it. We are shown things only when we are ready to find them.

Blend in with the crowd or do something unique, follow your dream or accept mediocrity, live or exist. We all, in some capacity, have the power of choice at our disposable and can change our direction in an instant.

If you need any inspiration then take a look at the countless stories of rags to riches, or the numerous people who have performed a u-turn from being a drug addict to the spiritually enlightened.

Embrace the many options available to you whilst taking the responsibility for your decisions and actions. I find it helpful to realise the impermanence of our existence, we have a limited and unknown amount of time here on Earth. We could be run over by a bus tomorrow, who knows? This thought makes me push myself and live life to the full, on my terms, and with the sole aim of being happy. Don't sabotage your dreams; create them, get them, find them, live them. If you have lost your thirst for life give yourself a good talking-to, never lose the precious gift of imagination, and remember that opportunities and experiences are yours if you want them badly enough. Just take the risk, change your **attitude,** change your **thinking,** and find the **motivation**. It is never too late.

11

Coming Out – Being You

♪ *I'm Coming Out*, Diana Ross ♪

Although this chapter is about how I burst out of the closet and how it shaped my life for the better, it is also about more than that. We all need to come out in our own way, and I don't mean by becoming homos (there wouldn't be much of a population if we did that!). You need to be true to yourself, and come out to the world as the real you. As I said in the first Lost Key, five things changed my direction in life and this was number three on that list.

As you will have gathered from previous chapters I grew up in a rural setting, in a small village close to a small town. My teenage years were spent in the 90s, people were tolerant of differences, but not as much as they are now, and less so in the Shire that I called home. I think I knew I was gay from about fifteen, I only say fifteen as that was the first age I can remember fancying a boy and not a girl. I was so scared about telling people, worried about what they would think, if friends would still be friends, and if my family would take it ok. Plus, if I am honest, I didn't really want to be gay, it seemed so abnormal.

I had never met any 'real gays', and I certainly didn't know any! As the years went by I ignored my crushes and went the other way by sleeping around with a handful of girls (not at the same time) as most guys in my year group did. I knew that they didn't mean anything to me or float my boat, but better to fit in than stand out I thought, especially given the number of tough pumped-up guys who would have made my life hell if I had had the courage to face my feelings then.

The dark days I experienced in my first months in London were cured by finding spirituality, a purpose, and by understanding the world and universe. But although I felt better, I still felt something else was missing, and I was working on that for a year afterwards. During that year I moved to my first houseshare (in South East London) and one night, out of total desperation and a feeling of hopelessness, I gazed out of my attic window with tears in my eyes, and begged and pleaded for the stars to give me a sign and some answers.

The next month one of the housemates moved out and a new one arrived, an Irish guy named Wesley had rocked up on our doorstep with his worldly possessions.

We had a connection the moment he moved in, his eyes would pierce mine when he was talking to me, and the energy between us was almost visible. I had friends staying over one weekend and gave them my bed to sleep in.

Wes said, "Bunk with me Toffy, rather than sleep on the sofa". We lay there for hours discussing our pasts, then, as he was walking to the loo, he said, "by the way, I am not exactly straight". With those words, he had ripped the carpet from under my feet, and turned my whole world upside down. I sat there in the dark knowing I couldn't go backwards into my life of denial. This guy was being open and honest with me about his sexuality, and I felt it was my chance to be honest with myself, and for the first time, with someone else.

He gave me the courage to come out, at first to friends and then to family. He told me his story, and how it had lifted an enormous weight off his shoulders. It was comforting to know all his friends including the more 'macho' ones had stuck by him. He told me how he could live the way he had always wanted, and no longer had to live a lie, and because of this was a much happier person. I knew it made sense, and I realised in that moment that my wish upon the stars had been answered in the form of an Irish leprechaun called Wesley. His timely arrival into my life was no coincidence by any stretch of the imagination.

I needed to be true to myself in order to feel at ease, and so I accepted I had no choice about my feelings or emotions towards the same-sex, it was just natural for me. I was gay.

A coming out story is not complete without me telling you how I told my Mum. As you will have read earlier in the book, she is a psychic, so it will come as no surprise that she was, well, not surprised. Laura (my lil sis) and I were at the village pub on Boxing Day with some of my friends. I had warned them that on the way home I was planning on telling Mum, who was also with us, that I was bi-sexual and not gay (to lessen the shock).

On the walk home I said, "Mum, I have something to tell you". She said, "go on" I replied, "I am bi-sexual" She said "No you are not, you are gay, who are you kidding?" That was it, after almost ten years of fretting, it was over in a second and she had known all along!

I can't express how much relief I felt after I admitted it to myself, and then to the people who were important to me. No one had an issue with me being gay, and compared to one gay friend of mine whose parents disowned him I suppose I was lucky. Strangely the guys I was most worried about telling were the ones who were most understanding. Boyfriends of my lady friends love the fact they know a 'gay'. I think it is the person they see and not the label, and that person is true to themselves, and not hiding anything. I am not trying to be butch or manly or anything else, I am just me.

I remember a night out with my mates of varying sexuality when we were chatting to a group of straight lads and the conversation got round to sexuality, and when they realised some of us were gay they loved it, they said they had never met any gays before and we were really nice, easy going, fun, 'sound' etc etc. Of course we are!

I wonder if the guys at school I was scared of would react in the same way now. To be honest, people can call me what they like; faggot, queer, homo, poof, gay-boy, bent, it doesn't really mean anything to me, because, well, I am all of the above (lol). I've only ever experienced homophobic abuse once. I was walking through Brixton late at night and a guy in a hoodie loudly shouted "poof' as he walked past me, and I laughed and shouted back "well spotted genius". Luckily, he decided not to knife me. It would have been like me shouting "hoodie wearer" at him. It means nothing.

I remember when Helen (my best friend who I stayed in Guildford with) asked me why I thought people were gay, as they could not procreate which is the instinctive reasoning behind heterosexual relationships. I had given this a lot of thought well before she asked me, and I replied, "As controversial as this may sound, I think it *could* be a form of modern day evolution. A natural process that occurred in some people in order to control the increasing population. The increase in the amount of openly gay people could well be a direct result of the overpopulation of our world, sometimes stemming from people who nowadays have fewer morals and more carefree attitudes when it comes to sex. This modern attitude of sex for pleasure and recreation can, and often does result in broken families, over-population, and a lack of natural resources for our rapidly growing race. You only have to look at places like China, with their one child policy because overcrowding has become so serious."

Before the days of contraception, and when religions

were practised by most of the population, couples had sex to have children and that was that. Since the lack of morals and perhaps lack of self-responsibility, the population has increased dramatically in such a short space of time that the planet is struggling to cope. So I concluded that maybe this natural feeling of attraction to the same sex is nature's way of evolving in order to control the population. Religious beliefs, moral obligations and responsibility once controlled reproduction in some shape or form, and as this has slowly vanished from society, something else has occurred in order to fill the gap.

I didn't say it quite as matter of factly or boringly as that, but you get the gist! Interestingly she has since 'come out' as a Lesbian. There must have been something in the water as my other best friend Thom is also gay – the three gay musketeers all from the same school and town, how very queer.

It takes great courage and honesty to know who you truly are as a person, for me, being gay is one part of that equation, for others it may be knowing and accepting that you are a sensitive person. If you 'come out' you will be free and able to express the real you.

Shortly after coming out, I was on a night out with my work group and I was drunk (no more than usual) and felt as free as bird, like the shackles had dropped from me. The next day a friend said our boss had asked her what was wrong with me, and said I seemed slaughtered! On that particular night I found myself tap dancing down the staircase of the bar, left leg over right leg, jazz hands a'shaking and singing, "New York, New

York" and I was also outrageously flirting with some of London's many gorgeous bar staff. I had been living a lie for twenty-one years, I was free and born again. I felt I deserved a little centre-stage for a while. Unfortunately it got mistaken for being paralytic! I soon got used to the feeling of freedom and packed in my theatricals!

I could bang on about fags and lezas, but ultimately, when I came out of the closet it changed my life for the better. I was able to live, act and be the person I felt I was. None of us are too old to be born again and start living more truthfully.

If there is something you are not being honest with yourself about, it will make you unhappy, so let it out and be true to yourself. You don't have to be gay to be happy, just be yourself, whatever that may be. Come out and be the real you, don't hold back, live what is inside of you, and feel the freedom of expressing your true self.

12
Part 1

Invisible Power – Love

♪ Can't Take That Away, Mariah Carey ♪

*I*RONICALLY THE LARGEST CHAPTER IN The Lost Keys is the one I am least qualified to write about – it is love. It is one of the biggest keys to finding happiness, and I see it as the fifth element on our planet after earth, air, fire, and water.

There are five parts to this Lost Key. Throughout part one I will use the term **Invisible Power** (IP). IP is the unexplainable **Spiritual essence or energy** that flows in and through all of us. To give an example, have you ever found that when you are with a particular type of person you can feel your energy being zapped? Or come away from a social situation feeling completely drained? This is because the other person has taken your IP from you and not given any in return.

When you are with friends, family, or work colleagues, have you felt that it can sometimes be fine and sometimes awkward? Have you met a person for the first time and naturally hit it off, or perhaps hated them? Well without trying to over complicate these strange occurrences I will share my view on why they happen.

I don't know if it's just me, and I don't want to sound big headed (I am really not that type of guy) but I feel confident I can change the whole dynamic of a group situation by how I interact or feel. If I am in a group situation, let's say with a group of people I have never met before on a work trip. I can actually feel the awkwardness and tension in the air and see it on their faces, and if I choose to sit there and let the atmosphere carry on it does, but if I make the conscious decision to get to know these people and enjoy their company, it happens, simple as that.

I have experimented with this theory in reverse when on a road trip with friends, and oddly enough it still happens. I told myself to lose interest and withdraw my interaction from the group. They all went from laughing and joking with loads of banter one minute, to silence and seriousness the next. This all happened because of the way I chose to interact or participate. Now that's just one person, deciding to change the dynamics. But imagine if all the people in a group were guarded, or didn't want to participate, surely it would result in an awkward situation and an uphill struggle for everyone involved?

Invisible Power is something that relates to the Spirituality of a person, the more Spirituality – the more IP. I also think the quantity of self-confidence plays a part in IP levels. You will naturally feel drawn to someone who comes across as confident or Spiritual. These people, and I count myself in this group (bet your thinking "of course you do"!), have high levels of IP that are visible to other people in many different ways that can't really be explained in words, or be seen with the naked eye. You just know they have something special about them, even if you just think they are very friendly or simply happy within themselves. I have been lucky enough to come across many of these people in my life, and I know straight away if they have this quality, a quality that has the ability to intrigue and draw others in.

So how did I get this seemingly constant stream of IP? Well I think we all have it within us from birth, but it just needs to be re-discovered and awoken. This re-discovery doesn't come naturally at first, it is a process of time and commitment to everything that I have mentioned in The Lost Keys. We all have the potential to be well-rounded happy people with lashings of IP, we just have to be on the right path. If you're reading this then you are already on that amazing, mysterious and awakening road and probably already have IP.

IP develops from an appreciation of life, an appreciation of all things on this planet, a respect for this planet, a genuine love for other people, a genuine concern for other people, an understanding of where you, the individual, fits into this world. Mainly it develops from having confidence within yourself about who you are.

Unfortunately most of the time the exchange of IP is more one sided than equal. This is because one person unconsciously or consciously wants more IP than they are giving. I can think of plenty of situations where I have found this happening to me. I won't name names at this point as it is showing the negative sides of certain people that I still hold dear to me, and I wouldn't want to immortalise their lack of awareness in this book. Having spent a whole weekend enjoying the company of 'Bert and Ernie', towards the end of Sunday – in a moment of quietness and calm (maybe seen to them as emptiness and awkwardness) – a conversation erupted about money and the situations we found ourselves in at the age of nineteen.

It started nicely and then changed into a session of dissing and fault picking with my life, belittling me and quite literally sucking up all the IP I had left in my being. It felt like I was being chipped away at, and left me feeling very empty and demoralised, much the same way as the Dementors feed off the happiness of their prey in Harry Potter. Looking back I think this was due to their lack of IP and self-confidence. In a moment of their weakness, under the influence of alcohol or not, they felt the need to put me down in order to make themselves feel better. At the time I was only at the early stages of my spiritual development and I was just beginning to grasp the New Age ideas so I was still hurt by what they said, and I couldn't quite understand the reason they had basically bullied me. I felt like my character, life, and personality had been assassinated in one fell swoop. It probably didn't help that I am such a sensitive soul as so many of us are nowadays.

That is one way in which I have felt my IP being robbed, but there are many ways it can happen. Can you think of any times when you have felt a similar feeling of sudden emptiness whilst in a social situation? Something that someone might have said verbally, or done non-verbally, that might have caused you to lose some of your IP to them? An obvious one is aggression. If someone is aggressive towards you, you can feel the change in power without question, and it doesn't have to be in the form of physical aggression either, verbal aggressive behaviour can cause just as much of a shift in power. One example of this is intimidation. It can be as subtle as someone talking too much and over-talking you, or as obvious as someone invading your personal space.

A different example I have experienced is when you are trying to communicate with someone, asking questions and trying to get to know them and it feels like a one sided battle. You can't seem to get through to them and they come across as very guarded when responding to your questions. I felt myself having to work extra hard to extract the simplest pieces of information from them. I came away feeling drained and exhausted which might have otherwise been a feeling of happiness in getting to know someone new. This was their method of receiving IP from me.

From observing world leaders in meetings, to listening to my sister Laura talking with her boyfriend

Steve, I can sense an exchange of power, an exchange of IP that is rarely 100% equal. Very few exchanges are 100%. You will know if it has been a largely unequal exchange, you just have to ask yourself if you feel less of a person, or exhausted. Do you feel as if you have given more than they have given? Was it an un-constructive conversation? If your answers are yes then it has been an unequal exchange.

If it is an unequal exchange, but just *slightly*, it should be comfortable enough for both people to sustain and this is how most exchanges take place. On the other hand if you happen to experience an **equal** exchange, bloody hell you will know all about it. It feels like a connection, like a meeting of souls and like you want to stay happily and comfortably in that situation for a long time.

With all types of social interaction you get back what you give out. That old Karma comes creeping back into play again, even in social situations! You can't expect to keep gaining energy and interaction from people if you're not willing to give some out yourself.

So after all my waffle about IP and examples of bad situations, the question is why do people steal IP, and how can we stop it? People like what they see (and are incapable of explaining) so they consciously or unconsciously take it from those that harness large quantities of it. By stealing this energy from another person they are taking something away, leaving that person with a feeling of emptiness. This results in nothing more than bad karma for the thieving mongrel.

Dipping in and out of this power is very bad for the Spirituality, and is not the most balanced way to live!

Eventually the IP thief begins to realise they are causing mental or perhaps even physical harm to the person they are stealing the IP from. Which in turn causes them to feel guilt or shame. Not good emotions for anyone to feel.

Note it next time it happens, and if you want to stop someone else doing it to you, then simply bring up the issue. As hard as it will be for you to bring it up, it will be twice as hard for them to hear a truth that they are effectively blind to. If this doesn't work then simply withdraw from the situation and don't give them what they are attempting to take from you – don't rise to the bait! There is another school of thought on this; that we should send them thoughts of pure love to raise their energy, or if you are feeling very vulnerable imagine a cloak wrapped around you – this becomes a shield from negativity. I haven't had chance to try these out, so I won't preach about them!

However, by far the best way to stop IP imbalances is to make sure we are not the ones stealing IP from others in the first place. That way we can cure the problem from the source. It will result in less people taking and more people giving. If you catch yourself doing it (highly likely for most of us at some stage in our life) then make a mental note and stop yourself in your tracks. I think it mostly happens when we feel awkward in a situation. Check you are not picking away at someone's IP to make yourself feel better – picking on them, withdrawing yourself, talking too much – whatever method it may be. Remember that it really isn't yours for the taking.

A warning to those people that keep on leeching

off others, or for those people who claim to like a good argument or confrontations; **you will constantly be in a loop of unhappiness**. By gaining a little bit of energy for each situation you are seemingly controlling, then losing it until the next time you attack your 'prey', you are only creating a vicious circle of continuing un-fulfilment. On top of this, people will choose to remove themselves from your company for fear of being targeted again. This will result in a very unhappy and lonely existence. *Cue the sound of Crickets!*

To put all of this a different way, and to make sure everyone reading this understands, here is a short more psychological way of explaining interaction and IP. People who are insecure with their own abilities, or insecure with their life having low self-esteem, pick-on and attempt to bring others down to their level to make them feel better about themselves or more comfortable in any given situation. These people move among us every day. They could take the form of the school-ground bully, dominating husband, ordinary friend, nagging wife, jealous sibling, or disagreeable work colleague. The methods they use vary as described already. Most of them probably aren't even aware they are doing it. The bottom line is we can't take IP from those who have more because it's not ours for the taking. Given time we will find our own source that we are capable of controlling. When that time comes you will realise it was worth the wait, and you will understand why it is so important to have a perfectly balanced exchange of IP during any form of interaction.

Next time you are in a social situation think about

your interaction in terms of both your physical and non-verbal actions. As you develop spiritually and find inner confidence you will be giving more IP out, and receiving equal amounts in return. Keep IP in the back of your mind and you will begin to see things in a different light. What you give out, you **always** get back.

12
Part 2

Compassion and Co-existence – Love

♪ *Proud, Heather Small* ♪

*L*OVE APPEARS IN MANY FORMS, but love for others is one of the most important types of love. Some religious guy once said "Thou shalt love thy neighbour as yourself", and what he meant by this was love everyone as you would yourself. That doesn't mean fancy them, or ask them out, it means love them for who they are, help them, feel their pain, and understand **we are all one of the same**.

During my first years in London when everything felt like an uphill struggle, I had contempt for everyone who got in my way on my commute to and from work. I didn't love my neighbours, and I really didn't want to either. I saw my fellow commuters as mere obstacles hindering what I thought should have been an easy journey to work. Other than the contempt I felt for these 'obstacles', I was also very critical about them. I would judge their appearance, and I would pick out their faults – everything from the colour of their socks to their hairstyles. By doing this I guess it made me feel better about myself on some shallow level. In actual fact I was only creating a negative kind of aura around me wherever I went, and it dawned on me that if I was judging them, then surely they had the right to judge me. This attitude acted like a vicious cycle of negative criticism even though it was just in my head.

Once I wised up to this, and when I voiced some of my criticisms in front of my Mum, she told me I had no right to judge others. The penny had dropped, I had to agree with her – I knew it didn't feel right every time I did it, and I knew it wasn't helping me at all. What made it ok for me to judge others? What gave me the right to criticise someone else's life, or for that matter their choices? Nothing – and I knew that.

At the end of the day we all seem very good at criticising other people's life choices but are not so good at looking at our own. If you catch yourself criticising others then note it, and put an abrupt stop to it. Try pinching yourself every time a negative thought arises. You will eventually get sick of the pinching and hopefully stop the negative thinking. Think of it as a form of conditioning.

As time went on and I began to understand the bigger

picture, I started to see that **everyone on this planet has a purpose** and we are all here to do something. From a homeless person on the street to the Prime Minister, from a starving person in Africa to a Banker – everyone shares the same thing – the air, the sky, nature, interaction, highs and lows, youth and age, laughs and tears, a desire to survive, a desire to be happy, a desire to be free from suffering and a desire to find an answer to the meaning of life. Whichever way you look at it, we are all in this life together as **ONE**.

We are all different, but all looking for the same things in life. We were born equal, granted we were born into different circumstances, some harsher than others, but we all have the same thing in common; an un-charted life ahead of us, to do more or less what we wish.

After meeting the Prime Minister for the first time I could see he was just like anyone else. I don't know why it surprised me, but for some reason I was under the illusion that Heads of State and Royalty were almost superhuman! Once the doors closed to the press (and I suppose closed to the outside world) he chatted away normally and was just the same as me in many ways (but not the gay part obviously!). Part of my job was to sleep at 10 Downing Street one night a week in case a crisis kicked off, or the PM needed some information on a particular subject. I would also take his Red Box up to his flat when I had finished preparing it. I saw the Prime Minister in very personal settings during my time there, and it turns out he is just a normal guy, trying to make a difference in the world.

We are all born, we all live, and we will all die. What we experience along the way is the only thing that makes us different from each other. It is up to each of us to decide how we <u>let</u> those things affect us.

We should all try to have unconditional love for every single person on this planet, but there are still some people out there who have an issue with race. I personally can't see why we ever had racists in the world, let alone in the 21st Century. It seems so immature and petty that people have issues with the colour of another person's skin. Does it really matter that someone is black, white or mixed race, in the grand scheme of things, does it really matter? Just because someone or something is different doesn't make it wrong or justify it becoming a figure of hatred.

I was stunned to find out we all originate from Africa. We are all related to those first human beings that evolved from the Ape family. From the African Plains our ancient ancestors pro-created and over the years emigrated outwards to Asia, Europe, India, the Americas and finally Australasia. They slowly populated the world as they explored new regions in search of food, space and resources. I was so amazed and happy to find this out. It shows that we really are related to each other, and have yet another thing in common as a human race. That is another reason why racism is a load of crap considering we are all from the same area and we share the same ancestors if traced back far enough!

We all co-exist and share the natural resources we have been blessed with, so it is about time we wised up and stopped racist behaviour. Perhaps back in the day it was a bit scary seeing another race for the first time, and when people are scared they generally react irrationally. But it's not like any of this is new anymore and therefore shocking or surprising. We are all, like it or not, sharing our cultures, heritage, traditions, and lifestyles with each other. I think it is a great way to experience the fullness of life, and this is especially true in the UK where we have a huge amount of diversity.

I would be the first to apologise for the *disgusting* behaviour of those who started the slave trade many years ago – but it's over, history cannot be re-written, so everyone involved has to move forward or be consumed by hatred towards people who no longer exist.

Other than racism, prejudice is another form of unnecessary hatred. Sadly I hear it sometimes in London, someone says "Bloody Paki's, coming over here getting all our jobs bla bla bla". I think they should put themselves in others shoes before making such sweeping statements. If the rest of their family lived overseas, or their life was in danger surely they would want to join their family or flee to another country? I know for a fact I would.

I find these narrow minded people are quick to judge. If they stopped to think, to relate to others more, they would find themselves with endless amounts of compassion and they would begin to understand the world and its contents on a much deeper level. By having love for your fellow inhabitants you begin to appreciate the important things in life, and by doing so you inevitably enjoy a happier outlook and mentality as a direct result of loving unconditionally.

If you can't see how this works yet then think about the opposite emotion – Hatred – if you hate every person you come into contact with, the direct result of this is a feeling of constant aggression leading to an unbalanced and unstable emotional state. Obviously these feelings of hatred will also provoke a response by those you come into contact with. I wouldn't want to be friends with someone who was aggressive all the time, and showed no sign of compassion or love towards me and others. Would you? **Hatred sends people running, love draws them in**. Try it. Try loving all people regardless of ridiculous things such as colour or religious beliefs. It is actually very easy to change your mind set with very little work.

To help someone in need is one of the most rewarding and satisfying things we can do. It probably won't cost anything either. I have a feeling we will help not just for self-gratification, but it will become a truly selfless act of altruism. An extreme example of this was my Mum's decision to look after a homeless lady (as her father had 50 years previously!).

She saw an old lady pushing a shopping trolley around the local village at one in the morning on a freezing night and pulled the car over to ask if she could help. The lady declined the offer the first time, but as winter approached and during another drive back from the village Mum pulled over and asked the same question. This time the response was more positive. The next day Hilary was sleeping in an old car we had at the front of the house and

Mum took her some food, water and clean clothes. Even though this homeless lady was very proud, she knew that Mum could help so she gave in and stayed with Mum for about two months.

As December got colder and colder Mum continued to plead with Hilary to come into the house and stay in the playroom that was rarely used. Eventually Hilary accepted and stayed there until January, cleaning the kitchen floor once in a while to "earn her keep" as she put it. During this time my Mum contacted the local paper who did an article on Hilary, asking if anyone had a spare caravan and a piece of land that Hilary could use. Sadly, although she was offered five caravans, there were no offers of any land to put one on. By the end of January, Hilary had vanished without any notice, venturing back onto the road with her trolley in tow. We felt very humbled by the faith she must have had to leave us with nothing but that trolley. Maybe this was the lesson.

This goes way beyond what most people would do to help another human being, but it shows that compassion exists and the lengths some people will go to help. I asked Mum why she did what she did, and she simply replied that if she was in Hillary's shoes (well not shoes as she didn't have any) that she would hope someone would do the same for her. Christ knows I hope someone would do the same for me.

Empathy is another fantastic quality that will help you see things more clearly and objectively. There are so many various ways to help others, anything from emotional support to volunteering at a homeless shelter.

Whatever you can manage or spare will go some way towards helping those in need, and by doing so you will also feel an accomplishment and satisfaction for helping. If you buy the Big Issue, regularly donate to charity, drop some old clothes off at a charity shop, or simply put a few pence in a collection pot you are helping, and it really does make a huge difference. Any one of us could have been born into situations a hundred times worse than our own. It's the luck of the draw. You could just as easily have been the homeless person on the street or the starving child in Africa.

I was in my flat one Saturday afternoon looking out over London, dancing round the lounge like an idiot, listening to some music, and singing into a hairbrush (just for the record I was sober). I realised then that I had some spare time on my hands! I wanted to do something fulfilling that would help others, so I decided to look up volunteering centres in South West London and see what was on offer. I signed up with a centre and I am still waiting to hear back from them about positions. It would appear that they are almost overstaffed with volunteers! How brilliant is that? It would seem there are too many people wanting to help, but I hope I will be able to give some of my time that was otherwise wasted badly singing, as Jen my flatmate can vouch, into a hairbrush on Saturday afternoons.

Throughout my lifetime I have seen celebrities endorsing and organising large events to raise awareness and money for the poor, helpless and starving people in third world countries. We need to look after these people in any way we can, through donations of our time, or donations of our money. We could be in their positions just as easily.

We can shut our eyes and turn our backs or we can realise it is happening; it is causing suffering and pain, and we can do something to help. Thanks to the media we can instantaneously see the devastating effects of things like the tsunami in East Asia, earthquakes in China, famines in Africa and hurricanes in the USA. These images hit me on a deep level and make me want to help. I feel for the starving children, the families that are torn apart, I feel for them as if they were my family or neighbours. It would seem that thou hath learnt to love thy neighbour after all!

Even if we all donated just £1, it would be enough to rebuild and send aid to these people that are so desperately in need. Individual donations lead to a collective power capable of *really* helping others.

We all want to be happy, and we don't want to suffer, so let's make a world where no one has to suffer emotionally, physically, mentally, or spiritually.

I have already mentioned the importance of love in religion, and how it seeps into most if not all religious texts and teachings. Without wanting to sound like I am living in the 60's ideology of free love and all that, **love is the most important thing we have on this planet**. We all have the ability to love, we all want to be loved by someone, and we can all experience love in many ways.

I have this deep down feeling that if we all loved each other unconditionally we would be living in a world free from suffering, war and famine. It will take time for everyone to realise that, and to put it into practice. But can you imagine a place where there is no fear or anger and only Love? It would be somewhere very special, and I hope it's not too far away.

Love everyone. Love everyone you have ever met, and everyone that crosses your path, even thou neighbour and thou enemies!

12
Part 3

Relationships & Their Ups and Downs – Love

♪ *Somebody That I Used To Know, Gotye* ♪

There are so many hundreds of explanations and theories behind attraction; from Freud to modern day psychologists. Love and relationships can be overcomplicated but I'll aim to keep it simples.

Love for a partner is just a basic attraction to another being on this planet that goes beyond the type of love I have already described. Once the attraction has formed, and if it manifests from desire into love then a special connection is formed between two

Spirits. Sometimes you just know that you have met an incredible person, and from such experiences I totally believe in love at first sight. It can start from something as small as an exchanged glance, to a full-blown conversation. You will know and feel something special when you come across it, it is an indescribable spark.

I am no serial lover as I have only been in a few serious relationships, but I want to share some of the main lessons I have learned. The most common reason relationships fail is because we see what we want to see in a potential partner. We have expectations about the other person, and once the honeymoon period is over and the veil of lust has dropped we realise they are not living up to those expectations. We try to change the person to fit our original view, and that is when arguments occur and fight for control begins. If we are able to accept a potential partner for who they are, without expectations and without wanting to change them, then a true and honest love can blossom which is based on sturdier foundations.

We have all either witnessed arguments, or perhaps experienced them within our own relationships. I myself have had the 'pleasure' of experiencing some arguments. The dynamics and workings of any couple involve some give and take. The more equal the process, the happier the couple, and the smoother the journey together. When you are in a relationship I think you are effectively **renouncing a 'you' and blending it to become a 'we'**. Instead of being two people you are almost joining to become one. That's why it is so painful when you split from someone you have been with for a long time; you are splitting something in half (it's all in the word)!

I have already described the IP battles within a group or social situation, but it also occurs in relationships – perhaps even more so. If both members of the couple aren't equally balanced with their spirituality and levels of IP (as most aren't) then it can turn into a battle for control and power.

One person or both will be fighting for the control of the relationship. It could be belittling each other, causing arguments for no reason, attempting to control the lifestyle of the other, attempting to make the other jealous, and the list goes on and on – but all of these methods are ways to take control of the other persons IP. In most heterosexual relationships it is usually the man that tries to take it all, but it happens nearly as often with the woman in any relationship. It really is no way to co-exist. Some people call it "wearing the trousers" others call it "under the thumb". They both sum up the unequal balance of IP in relationships.

Instead of trying to take away your partners IP, add to it. Send them positive thoughts and energy. If this process is **equal** then both of you will fill up with an all-encompassing feeling of love and Spirituality beyond anything you will have experienced before.

If you are attempting to control someone you supposedly love, then you are changing the very person you fell in love with. You cannot start a relationship with a person then try and change who they are unless they have asked for specific help in changing. Otherwise, we would be no better than dictators. Plus, after you had created your 'perfect partner' they would no longer be the person you fell in love with. Given time you will realise you are no longer in love with your Frankenstein creation.

Before you enter a relationship you need to know who **you** are, and what **you** stand for. Far too often I see people running from relationship to relationship looking for something; something they cannot find within themselves. It's so sad to watch, knowing that they will never be satisfied until they work on themselves.

So while you're in a relationship, try really hard to keep your individuality whilst at the same time becoming one and respecting each others differences. Don't lose sight of who you are and what you stand for. Once you have learnt how to increase and maintain your own IP, and your partner has done the same, you will find the relationship will flourish as it should – **perfectly balanced and perfectly equal**, all the while enjoying the companionship and love of another being. Go out with your friends, let your partner do the same with theirs, and have separate interests as it all makes for a healthy relationship. Also tell the truth to each other. Lack of trust is one of the main problems in relationships.

Towards the end of one of my relationships I found myself getting jealous, and on one particular night when we were on holiday I remember going mad because Wes was talking to a guy in a club. I stormed out and went back to the hostel. The whole way back I was building it up in my head as something terrible and evil. I felt betrayed, hurt, and used. Eventually Wes turned up and I went off on one, saying how could you chat him up in front of me like that, it's so rude bla bla bla.

Then I realised what I was feeling was a thing called jealousy. I said this to Wes. Then I asked myself why I felt jealous, and the reason was my own insecurity – I felt like I wasn't good looking enough to keep him anymore, that there was nothing keeping us together. This was where the jealousy stemmed from. I said all of this openly, we talked it over, I apologised and vowed to always tell the truth about my feelings – jealousy didn't invade our relationship again! Be honest with yourself and each other, it really will help.

There seems to be two ends of the spectrum when it comes to relationships. At one end you have people who are missing bits and pieces, attempting to take it from their partners (more destructive and likely to end very quickly and painfully), and on the other end, you have the two wholes idea (rare to find); making a perfect relationship without much effort.

And somewhere in the middle of these two you have my "two halves makes a whole" theory. If you find someone that is missing "something" and you yourself are also missing or lacking "something" there's a chance the two of you can connect and help each other become two "wholes" instead of two "halves". Both destined to meet in order to help each other. This is the middle way in relationships, and probably the most constructive of the three. The help must be equal on both sides for it to work, but if equal it can be a fantastic experience. This help doesn't necessarily mean sitting down and talking things through, it could be through non-verbal actions or on a much deeper spiritual level. My sister Laura and her boyfriend Steve have this kind of understanding, although they probably don't realise it. Laura used to be very shy and Steve is very confident. He has shared this on some level with her, and she has developed as a result. Steve used to talk a lot when he felt uncomfortable in situations and I have noticed that over time this is diminishing, something Laura has no doubt taught him in one way or another.

I think the same applies to friends we meet. Most people we come across can help our personal development, just as we can help theirs. For it to truly work the exchange must be equal. What a great way for everyone to develop!! The most important factor in any relationship is that sharing has to be **<u>100% equal</u>**.

Wherever you are on the relationship spectrum, if you are having doubts about the suitability of your partner ask yourself if they are the right one for you, **trust that your heart will tell you the honest answer**.

Relationships take work, don't be a fool and believe they should be an easy ride (excuse the pun). Don't settle for second best either. One of my golden rules has always been **NEVER SETTLE**. I have refused to settle for anything less than I deserve, but as I get older, living by that statement seems more difficult, probably because I am worried I will be left on the heap at thirty five. I still refuse to settle, and will live by that. I spent four years as a singleton because I followed that golden rule, and I do not regret it all, as I learned lots and lots in the process.

I refused to be with someone else, living in unhappiness just for the sake of it.

One thing in particular that I want everyone to remember is not to be afraid to enter new relationships. It is so easy to get hurt or downtrodden after a failed relationship but the key is to think positive. I have seen people break down after their relationship has ended. It seems their whole life has stopped. I have been there too, and although I have always been the one to end relationships, it still hurts. It hurts so much, and you play everything over in your mind, you think about second and third chances but there comes a point where you HAVE to realise that you are not compatible.

If you are not happy, and there is no chance of working at it, then you get out. Most people I have spoken to who are fresh out of a long-term relationship always say the same thing "I should have known, the signs were there." I ask the same question "I bet you were sleeping back to back every night towards the end" The response is always "yes!" So read the signs, do something about it, be bold, be brave and follow your heart.

I split from a boyfriend of eleven months, which in 'Chris Years' is like three years. Towards the end I found myself lying awake next to him, thinking about our differences and how I couldn't carry on anymore. I even had to sleep on the floor at the end of the bed once as I just couldn't sleep near him (not because he was at fault, just because I felt so uncomfortable). It still took me another month to break it up. We had made plans, holidays, and my head was telling me to stay put, my heart was telling me to bite the bullet.

We were different people, wanted different things, and had different priorities in life. I didn't want to hurt him, but then it dawned on me (as selfish as this sounds) that I was unhappy, and my happiness had to come before his. I met him at a pub, and he said he knew 'it' was coming. He graciously agreed with me and said he knew he couldn't change my mind. I left and went to see some friends for support. I jumped on the tube, headed into town and put my Ipod on, and guess who started to play? – Adele. Now I love the gal, in fact I would love to go on a night out with her, but I don't recommend you play her following a break-up, especially as you're travelling in rush hour. I had a few strangers ask me if I was ok as tears involuntarily dripped down my cheeks. I was pretty sure I had made the right decision, but as it felt like such a 'split of two souls' (as it does in most break-ups) I wasn't 100% sure. A week passed and I realised I felt more free and happier again, and that was proof enough that I had made the right decision.

The above person was a great guy, as was Wes. They both came into my life at the right *moment* in time, for the right *amount* of time, and they taught me things I needed to know about life and myself, as I did them. However, something inside of me knew they were not 'The Ones'.

I refused to settle, so I had to move forward and continue my search for that one person I genuinely wanted to spend the rest of my life with. How do we know when we have found that one person? I think we just have to trust our feelings on that one. That is the beauty of failed relationships, they help you work out what you want, and maybe more importantly what you *don't* want from future ones.

During my four years of singledom I dated plenty of guys and I always gave them a second date as I felt the first one was like an interview with the added bonus of wine. A few of the luckier ones made it to a fourth date, and even at that early stage I would ask myself if that was the person I could imagine spending the rest of my life with. The answer was usually no. I just could not be with someone I didn't see a future with, or did not feel happy with. You have to be selfish when it comes to relationships, selfish in the sense that you deserve the best, regardless of how old you are, or if your biological clock is ticking. Be honest with yourself.

Don't take issues from past relationships with you into the next one. Deal with them beforehand. Don't take failed relationships too personally either, trust that it isn't meant to be if they didn't work out. We usually find our next love when we are not looking, don't be desperate and just be you. People are attracted to truth and confidence, live true to yourself, don't be something you are not, and be confident. I must use the "f" word again – FAITH. Have FAITH in the master plan, trust that there will be someone more suited and better for you waiting around the next corner. As you shut one door another one will open. Believe in that, and it will see you through any emotional pain you are experiencing. So *what* if you get hurt again? It is worth the risk, and you won't know if you don't try. The next one might be **THE ONE!!**

Love can be the most amazing experience in your lifetime, or it can be the most unstable fluctuating emotion you will ever have. You have the ability and power to choose.

12
Part 4

Family Life & The Importance of You – Love

♪Video, India Arie ♪

ANOTHER FORM OF LOVING IS the love we have for family and our children. I don't have any children, but I have a gorgeous godson Jake and have seen Mum's Foster children grow up from young kids. I have seen how much love is poured into them as they grow up. They constantly need attention and love forms a huge part of their development, if not the main part.

I believe a lack of this kind of love is the sole reason many people have issues when they get older. They feel as though they didn't receive enough love or support from their parents when growing up.

For those of you that do not have children but want them, I think it is so important to want them for the right reasons. I was having this discussion with a friend a while back. We were saying that it's disgusting that some people can have children who really don't deserve them, and those people that want children more than anything in the world aren't able to. We were suggesting that there should be some kind of test you have to sit before you are eligible to have children, but I was saying that it takes away the fundamental right of everyone to procreate and would mess with our freedom. It's a tricky one.

When our society had more morals and values, people only had children when they were in a marriage and generally when they were able to support themselves financially. Now, everywhere you look you see teenage girls having babies, supporting them with benefits, or living at home with their parents. They feel a sense of aggression for their youth being cut short, and for being so financially unstable. This is no way to bring up kids. The children will grow up with issues directly related to the environment they were brought up in. No doubt repeating their parent's mistakes and turning into what some people would call yobs. Of course there are exceptions to this rule, but without giving true unconditional love to a child there isn't much hope of them ever reaching their full potential.

I think the people that have kids for purely selfish reasons should give it a second thought, not least because of all the work involved in raising a child. What I find very hard to understand is when people have children to fill a gap in their own life. I once heard someone say that they wanted kids to receive the unconditional love that children have for their parents. I was very shocked and thought it was unbelievable.

To bring life into this world is a precious gift most of us are lucky enough to have, but to do it to fill a void in your life is simply not what it's all about. **You** have to fill that void and work out your issues yourself, not by creating a **temporary solution** through an **external** source, and definitely not if that temporary solution is in the form of a human life. If you have expectations that your child will fill a void, the poor kid will fundamentally be just that, something to fill a gap in your life.

If on the other hand you want children for the right reasons then it can be a truly amazing experience for both parent and child. I was lucky enough to have been raised in this world by my lovely Mum, and I am 100% sure that my parents decision to have me was for purely selfless reasons. After my Mar and Par got divorced when I was about six, my Mum gave us enough love for both parents. I have never felt as if I needed more from a second party, which I think is an incredible achievement and something I am eternally grateful for. I have love for her, my sisters, brother, aunt, uncle, gran, grandpa (when he was alive), cousin, and nephew. They have all been around for different amounts of time during my lifetime, seen my progression from childhood to adulthood, and they have shaped my life in ways that I could never try and pinpoint. It was only at my Granddad's funeral that I realised this. I kind of always knew it, but it wasn't until it was spelt out for me that it hit home. Uncle John was reading a eulogy about Grandpa, and as he read aloud I began to see similar characteristics in both my Mum and myself. From small things about his love for animals, to feeding a homeless person that was staying in one of his hay barns. I turned to Mum and said, "That sounds familiar!" His actions, behaviours, and ethics have spread down the family tree through my Mum to me, I feel so privileged that these were all good aspects and not violence or aggression. It shows how much influence we have over successive generations. I am sure Grandpa would never have guessed how much influence he would have over me when he first considered having kids with my Gran.

That's another reason to think twice about having kids, because your actions have so much impact on not only them, but also their children, and their children's children, and the innumerable people they come into contact with during their lifetimes. One wrong move by a parental figure could set a path of destruction in motion for future generations. Take Hitler for example, I bet his grandparents hadn't expected that their actions would lead to the death of millions. One action could set or change the course of the entire future, for good or bad. That's a lot of responsibility to take on.

The negative actions of parents can be broken, and that's just one of the many benefits of the spiritual times we find ourselves in. We have all been gifted with the ability to change our future at any given moment, regardless of our past and regardless of the influences we were subjected to whilst growing up. My old flatmate

Jen and I went to watch a 'Black' drama in East London that a friend of mine was stage-managing. It was about bringing up children and family life in the 21st century. What hit me was the amount of people who related it to their own lives.

I heard a group of twenty year old cockney guys saying "Yea man, that was really some'ink, want me Mum to come watch this. You knaa what? I am gonna break da cycle, I am gonna be da one to do it, ya get me?" That theatre production had hit them on a deep level and had provoked a positive reaction, and it got me thinking how lucky I was with my upbringing. I know there are people out there who are not so lucky, and have been abused verbally or physically. But just as those guys said, you **can** break the cycle. All it takes is for one generation to have the realisation and the motivation to change it. Above all, as the saying goes; you can choose your friends but you can't choose your family. I am glad to say that I wouldn't choose another, even if I could.

Be aware that you are born into your family circle for a reason, so learn from them, and they will learn from you. Help each other, try and find the reasons that, out of the entire world, out of the entire population of this globe, you have ended up with your particular family unit. It is not just a coincidence – that would be a bloody massive coincidence!!

I have outlined the main types of love so far, but the most important is **Love for yourself**. If you don't have love for yourself then how can you love others without any expectations? Loving yourself is the first step towards a perfect relationship, and the first step in loving others.

If you love yourself, then no matter what anyone does to you or tries to inflict upon you, you cannot be affected. By loving yourself you have an internal strength that cannot be broken.

I remember this was one of the main things Mum drummed into us when we were kids, *especially me*. She would always say, "Chris, you should love yourself more", never explaining what type of love she meant. I took it to mean my appearance and I turned out to be very vain! I am still trying to rectify that little misunderstanding.

Ultimately though, I know I love myself minus the vanity. I love who I am, and what I stand for. I have a confidence within myself that is unshakable and roots me to this planet like a tree to the ground. By knowing who I am I appreciate every little thing from the walk to work, to those blissful quiet moments I spend alone without distractions. Love for yourself should start from within, loving who you are and what you stand for, and then radiate outwards to your physical body. When I was younger I was just pre-occupied with the external side of myself.

Learn to be happy with whatever you were blessed with. If your appearance hasn't changed because of external influences like overeating then you should be safe in the knowledge that you were born that way (Lady Gaga said it so well), and that's just who you are. You cannot do anything about it so accept your lot from life. The variety of people on this planet is incredible, and we are all different and attractive inside and out in our own special ways. Don't forget it. Instead of picking the negative aspects of yourself, why not change your attitude and pick out the positives, it's a far nicer way to evaluate yourself, and takes less energy and emotions!

One of the worst failings of the NetGen is our tendency to compare ourselves to everyone around us – celebrities, models, friends or just Joe Bloggs in the street. I occasionally still do, but I am slowly trying to change my mindset because it cannot bring anything other than jealousy and ultimately unhappiness. When I catch myself looking at all the incredibly buff and model-like guys at Sainsburys on Clapham High Street (more of a catwalk than a supermarket) I say to myself; "if we all looked the same, we wouldn't know beauty and appreciate differences", and, besides, everyone has their own ideals of what beauty is anyway. What one person thinks of as attractive, another person will find unattractive. Looks and appearances are only superficial, inner beauty and personality will always outshine our external shells. And that is not something just ugly people say!!

12
Part 5

The Power of Music & Conclusion of The Fifth Element – Love

♪ *THE HEART ASKS PLEASURE FIRST, MICHAEL NYMAN* ♪

MANY OF THE SONGS THAT have been in the music charts over the last decade feature love heavily. There are more and more frequent references and whole songs about loving each other regardless of race, religion etc, and coincidentally they have done *really* well. I think that is because the lyrics in the songs strike a chord with us on some deeper level. Michael Jackson, Adele, Jack Johnson, Kelly Clarkson, Black Eyed Peas, Madonna,

Kanye West, even Eminem – they are just a few artists I can think of that fit this category. I have also seen an increase in the popularity of relaxing soul-touching music like Enya, Enigma, and Buddhist Chillout type music, which shows a huge shift in society's attitude towards all things spiritual. When I was a teenager most people saw this sort of music as mumbo jumbo hippy music. At the time, I would happily go to bed every night listening to the sounds of the whales and dolphins or Enya, and on the rare occasions my friends did stay over at the 'Witches Lair' they thought it was really nice relaxing music.

A spot of history for you – I never realised until recently that music is one of the oldest forms of communication. It stretches right back to the Neanderthals who once lived in caves. Also in the early periods of time it was used by Aboriginals in Australia for tribal rituals, the Native Americans for spirit incarnations, and it was used in meditations in ancient Tibet. I think that's quite telling really. Music has been with us for as long as humans have existed.

Music has in the past united us for good deeds. It is a truly universal language and can touch us on a spiritual level. Sometimes I hear a piece of music and I feel tingles down my spine and can lose myself in the notes or by dancing to the rhythm. I have debated putting the following sentence in, but I will, as I don't have anything else to hide and if you think I am a lunatic, so be it! – When I am home alone, I find a piece of music that uplifts me, usually some form of trance music where the music starts off slow and gradually builds into a euphoric crescendo, and I dance like a maniac. I just go with the rhythm and aim to feel it in my soul and do whatever comes to mind regardless of what I look like. It is so invigorating, and I am sure it must set-off happy signals in my brain. At Christmas I was running around a field in the Shire, in the arctic conditions, when my favourite trance song came on. I screeched to a stop and danced under the moonlight until the song had finished. That moment was the most amazing experience, and both free and easy to do. Try it for yourself, dance sober to your favourite music and feel a quality of ecstasy and love rush through you.

Music speaks to me. I love that it can remind me of situations, people or emotions. I love it so much that you will have noticed I put a song to each chapter of this book! X Factor gets me every year, I love that people are achieving their dreams and are communicating their emotions through singing. The urban family and I have shed tears on many occasions when watching the auditions. The ones that set us off are the people who are not just singing beautifully, but the people who use personal experiences to make the songs come to life. The video and song from Sinead O'Connor, "Nothing Compares to You" is a classic, and she does just that. Apparently she was thinking of her deceased Mum when she sang it. It is such an emotionally stirring video and touches others because she makes it personal.

There have been a few occasions over the last couple of decades when Pop artists clubbed together to produce charity songs. The words, images and messages behind them have been hard-hitting, and the profits have helped so many people, including those in third world countries. The publicity behind these songs does help, but the words coupled with well-written music hits home. I think it's so good to see celebrities using their status for positive reasons. The same applies for all the charity concerts, they bring people together for a common purpose and the music reaches out and touches so many, even if they don't speak the same language. You only have to look at the Make Poverty History and Band Aid songs as prime examples.

Music is just one example of our deep routed awareness of love. If you have ever been to a concert and felt the power and vibe of the crowd and performance you will know what I mean. The artist is giving the crowd their gift through sound, and in return the crowd shows focus and appreciation through clapping. This results in a balanced and reciprocal exchange of energy that raises everyone up into a state of euphoria, especially if that particular music hits the individuals on a deep level.

The great composers of the music world like Beethoven produced such amazing music because they wrote it from their souls. They believed it was their purpose to provide the world with music that would stir emotions and uplift the soul. Great music can conjure all sorts of emotions and feelings, and have a positive effect upon a listener. That is the sign of a true musician. The same goes for all artists, musical or otherwise. I think it is their souls purpose to produce something that awakens emotions or a form of spirituality in others.

I believe we all have a purpose on this planet to do what we believe is within us. Some might be passionate

Carpenters, others Clothes Designers, Teachers, or Writers. It just takes a bit of time to tap into our individual talents to realise our soul's purpose. Once you find it you will know, it will come naturally and you will enjoy doing it more than anything else, and you will likely be a leader in that particular field if you find the motivation to follow your dream.

A final note; like music, we are all made of atoms and particles that vibrate. There are types of music and notes that vibrate at a certain level capable of balancing our own frequency levels. Some music can change our own levels for the better. Tibetan singing bowls are just one example. They are made of copper and rounded like a large mixing bowl. You place them in your hand and strike it with the wooden beater or roll it around the edge of the bowl to create a perfect tune that you can actually feel vibrating on your hand. I find it completely relaxes me, and I have this image pop into my head that the vibration causes a rippling through my body correcting any imbalances. It's very strange, but seems to work a treat!

The harmonising effects of sound can fill us with a feeling of peace and love if used correctly. In the future I envisage people visiting some form of acoustically engineered chamber for sound healing. Various sounds, notes, tones and pitches will be played, designed to harmonise the atomic structure of our bodies.

So I'll wrap it up there and conclude this lengthy but most important of Lost Keys:

1. Enjoy and use music. Find a type of music that uplifts you, makes you feel good and feel the

benefits of dancing to the sounds. Absorb the notes into your very being and imagine it transforming your atomic make-up for the better!

2. Learn to love yourself. Love yourself internally and externally, making sure you have a balance between the two. Spend time evaluating who you are, if you're not happy with some aspects of yourself then change them.

3. Love and learn from your family, biological or not. We did not choose how we were raised, so you have to appreciate the lessons and teachings that you were subjected to. For those with dysfunctional families your lessons might be to learn from the mistakes of your family, bettering yourself, and passing that on to your children. Or it could be that you are supposed to help change the mindsets of your family and help them with their issues. There are lessons in every part of life; you just have to look hard enough, and sometimes read between the lines in order to find them.

4. Love your partner with no expectations, and don't enter a relationship with any. Aim to love unconditionally. Unconditionally meaning with no conditions, limitations, or provisos attached – this is the most stable way to sustain a relationship. If you don't think you can do that then you are probably not ready for a relationship and need to take more time working on yourself, by yourself.

Once you are ready, give IP equally and be honest with each other. The lack of honesty and not talking about how you feel are the biggest sources of arguments – you can't read each other's minds (yet!), so by speaking honestly, you do away with assumptions and accusations. Never try to control another person.

5. Love others who you meet in your lifetime. By doing so you will attract the right sort of people into your life. Have compassion and empathy for all you come across. We are all equal on so many levels, and you could have easily been the beggar on the street.

6. Don't steal IP in social situations. Be aware of how you act and react in such situations. If you catch yourself taking IP from others (by any of the various means) stop yourself in your tracks. Build up your own IP through spiritual practices, by knowing who you are, and what you stand for.

7. **Finally, think loving thoughts.** Pinch yourself when you have negative or critical thoughts.

13

Six Feet Under~ Death

♪ *Candle in the Wind*, Elton John ♪

*T*HERE COMES A POINT, WHERE life stops giving us things and starts taking them away. I have experienced one death in my circle of friends, and two in my family. But oddly, the first death that affected me was a lady I had never met before. Her name was Princess Diana, and her death back in 1997 really struck me. We were living in a log-cabin house positioned by the river on stilts, and I was playing on our rope swing with Laura when Mum told us that Princess Diana had died. It didn't really mean much at the time, but when we watched the funeral footage a week later it somehow hit home. I cried throughout most of it, and really felt for Prince William and Harry. My first pet (a chinchilla called Rosie) had died three years earlier but this somehow felt different. I think I was finally realising that humans were impermanent and nothing lasts forever. Elton John's song "Candle in the Wind" still gets me now. It felt like the whole country was in mourning for the loss of the lovely Lady Di.

The first more personal death I experienced was many years later. Jenna was a really close friend of mine from school. We bounced off each other and had exactly the same sense of humour. I remember our first meeting really well. I was in the common room at the start of Year Ten and she was with some of our mutual friends. Jenna had an amazing infectious smile, and a natural light that sort of shone from within. She came over and introduced herself telling me about a funny lesson they had just had together and we soon became close friends. We never did much work in lessons because we were always laughing about stupid things and getting each other into trouble. 'It' happened after about a year of knowing her. One night she went out and took half an ecstasy pill with some of her friends, and from what I gathered it was her first time. As quickly as she had come into this world she left – the ambulance crew couldn't resuscitate her.

I got a phone call from her friend saying she had some bad news and I should sit down. I instinctively knew what she was going to say, but it was still a huge shock. She asked me to ring round the people I knew, which I reluctantly did. Afterwards I went to the local park, lit up three cigarettes and smoked them all at the same time, lined up in a row in my mouth. I sat on the swing just smoking and crying whilst looking up at the clouds and asked "Why, why her, and why so young?" I kind of believed in a God back in those days and I was angry at him/her/it for taking such a lovely, caring and fun loving girl.

Looking back now I think I was too young to understand death, and so I just accepted it as best I could. I went to her funeral and said my goodbyes. It was very emotional and I saw firsthand what death does to a family and close friends. We all loved her so much and then she was gone forever, just like that. I couldn't watch her burial, it was too final, and far too traumatic. At the time I wasn't sure if there was a heaven, but from attending that first funeral I knew it brought closure. In such circumstances, closure seems very important, although strangely surreal. My heart goes out to people who lose someone and never discover what happened to them.

The second death I experienced was my Granddad's in 2007. I am sure you will have gathered from reading some of the other Lost Keys that I am very close to all my family. My Grandparents would visit us once a week when I was younger. We regularly meet up for birthdays and other events, usually about fifteen of us in total. We are the family in the corner causing havoc with the menu ordering. We ask for things that are not on the menu and then later you will find each of the adults fighting to pay the bill, throwing cards at the waitress begging her to put it all on one card. The winner takes all in this game!

After six weeks of illness my Granddad passed away. It was relatively sudden, although I think we all knew it was inevitable as he had terminal cancer. There was a period of slight hope, but without wishing to sound negative, I knew his time was up. He was a wonderful role model of compassion and love. During his short stay in hospital whilst seriously ill, he would ask us to do various things for the other patients that the nurses had no time to do and he had noticed were upsetting them. When my Mum told him she had 'seen' his deceased Mother at the end of a lane smiling and waving – he replied, "I will be alright then". A week before he died I wrote a few words about death, and about his life with the intention of reading it at his funeral. After he died I showed it to my Mum and she thought it was a lovely idea and encouraged me to find the confidence to read it aloud at the service.

I saw Gramps' death as a **celebration of his life** rather than a **commiseration of his death**. This phrase almost seems cliché now-a-days, but I fully believe in it. He was lucky enough to have lived a full and varied life, whilst at the same time having the state of mind of someone much younger than his eighty-six years. I could understand my family's reasons for being upset at his death, of course I could, especially my Gran's, after all they had been married for 65 years, but I didn't feel particularly upset myself. I would like to say that was because I had evolved spiritually enough to realise that **death is as certain as birth**, that it is something that will happen to every single one of us without a question of a doubt, but it was more likely that it was because he was old when he died.

I often wonder if I would have felt the same way about my young school friend if I had the same awareness then, as I do now. Who knows? Shortly before his death, he told my Mum there were three men in the kitchen waiting to take him with a clock above their heads reading 11:00. He was always asking us the time after this, and we are sure he made a pact with 'them' as he was pronounced dead at 11:02 five days later!

With Gramps' death I felt comfortable that he had ridden the course of life and his time was up. Although personally tailored to my Granddad's life, I want to include the words that I read out at his funeral as it sums up my ideas and feelings of death.

"A Celebration of life"

I want to say some words about Gramps. This is the first death I have experienced in my family, and although we hear this phrase often, I truly believe that death should be a celebration of life, and not the end of a life.

From the moment we are born there is one thing that is absolutely certain, we will all die at some point. It's an equal but opposite reaction, like everything else in the world. It is a 'dead cert' as Gramps might have said about one of his horse bets!

I really think Gramps had an amazing life, and he did so much with all of his many gifts. Gramps was a man of great intellect, which was equalled by his fantastic if not dry sense of humour. I still laugh when I think of all the times Gramps met friends of mine, he would always call them a completely different name to their introduction! My Friend Thom was nicknamed "The Pipers Son".

My friends would probably get the impression he was old and past it. As we all know Gramps was streets ahead of many at his age and a member of MENSA. There was never a single time I can remember asking Gramps a question, without him knowing the answer. He would also make quick-witted funny comments to random people, much to Gran's embarrassment, but I noticed she would always have a little chuckle!

The Gramps I knew in my lifetime was as happy sitting back and absorbing all the chit chats of a family get together, as he was actively engaged in an intellectual conversation, or a sports debate.

He practically taught himself to use his mobile phone including texting Alex for Cricket updates. One afternoon at work I found an email from none other than Albert Kirby, saying he had cracked it and was testing his email. I don't think much got the better of Gramps throughout his life. I used to love listening to his stories of him when he was a young lad in the war, and it made me realise how much he lived life and saw of the world.

This man you may know as a friend, as Gramps, as Daddy, or as your Husband; was a man with great patience, a man with great knowledge, a man with a kind heart, and a man that has had a positive effect on all of us sitting here today. Thank you Gramps for simply being you."

As I read this to the seated congregation I didn't feel an ounce of sadness. I only cried when I saw the reaction on the faces of my Gran, Aunt, Sister, Brother, Cousin and Mum. That's when it hit me; even though fundamentally, death is nothing to be frightened of, or upset about, it still touches people in many different ways. Attachment is formed from love (which is no bad thing), but when the time comes we must all be prepared for it and let them go with love.

From both of these deaths (I deliberately won't use the word 'loss' because I find that a selfish term) it made me realise the importance of life, and how short it is. **Because it is so short, and because we only get one shot at it, it's important not to think too much about the future or the past, as that wastes the present moment.** The present is often forgotten as we go about our daily life, but it is something that is very important. **You can't change the past and you have relatively little influence over the future, but you are living in the present all of the time**.

The death of my school friend really highlighted this to me. It can happen to any of us, **at anytime**. By realising the uncertainty of our lives it puts everything else into perspective, like stupid arguments with loved ones or complaints about the weather – it's really not that important. Ask yourself if, in six months time, it will have any relevance!

I lived and worked in Iraq during some of the most dangerous times of the post-war clear up. Before I departed I was sent for a week's security awareness training in Wales. The course was run by a couple of ex-SAS Officers who taught us how to avoid kidnapping, gunfire, bombs, and how to administer emergency first aid whilst under attack in war zones. The course basically raised our awareness to another level, heightened our senses and exposed us to the very real dangers of working in hostile regions. Before arriving in Wales, I saw my posting to Iraq as a way of paying off my debts, and shaking up my routine, boring life. When I left Wales I realised what I had let myself in for – possible death! Still, the whole decision was my choice and I stuck by it. I had all my belongings put into storage, held a camouflage-themed leaving party, downloaded the song Highway to the Danger Zone from Topgun to play on the way into Iraq, packed my body armour and I was ready for the off.

Wes (my boyfriend at the time) and Thom came with me to Heathrow. They were both crying as I waved goodbye to them at the security line, which of course started me off. Thoughts like, "what if I never see them again" went through my head. I shook it off and went directly to the BA Business Class Lounge (work had the decency to fly us Business Class to Kuwait) downed a few bottles of Bollinger champagne and boarded the plane.

I was somewhere over the Middle East when I decided to read a letter from Wes that he had given me at the airport. He wrote about how much he loved me, that he didn't want me to go, that I had changed his world, and was telling me to keep alert and not put myself in dangerous situations. Again I cried my eyes out, realising that I actually was on a highway to the danger zone. I passed out watching some rubbish movie and woke up as we were coming into land, I looked out of the window to see no fields, but huge areas of sand and dust (the first I had ever seen) which still makes me grateful the UK has rain.

Before I had left the UK I was told a man in a white shirt with black stripes on his shoulder would meet me by Starbucks in arrivals. He wouldn't be holding a name board to avoid any potential kidnap threats or hostile government attention (spies, being followed, bugged, the usual). I found him, wondered for a minute if there was some secret phrase I should be asking him and then we were off on the 45 minutes drive to the American Airbase.

Our incoming military plane had been delayed due to a sandstorm so I had to wait in a hot tent for seven hours with young soldiers laughing and joking like it was the most normal thing in the world. When we finally boarded, I was surprised to find the "seats" were actually thick cargo-type nets positioned the whole length of the plane, facing each other, with harness seatbelts. I sat down near the front of the plane, opposite a cocky loud young soldier who looked at me as if to say "you are on the wrong flight mate". I stood out like a sore thumb in my desert boots, combats and long-sleeved t-shirt. I put on my body armour and helmet, plugged in my ipod and was ready for my adventure.

I could barely hear my ipod turned to full volume over the sound of the engines. As we entered Iraqi airspace the Pilot turned off the lights, illuminating me (the sore thumb), and all of the soldiers in an eerie greenish glow cast by the emergency lights. The faces around me turned sober, the cocky soldier was now a young boy who looked no older than seventeen. The mood turned tense, and after just ten minutes I saw what look liked fireworks explode outside the small porthole windows, and we heard a muffled bang. The plane manoeuvred a hard right, and, I shit you not, just at that moment my chosen song Highway to the Danger Zone decided to play on my ipod. My ipod has a habit of playing inappropriate songs. Its ironic charm was lost on me on this occasion though, and for a fleeting moment, I thought it was all over. What the hell was I thinking downloading that song? Did I think it would be fun in Iraq, a game, a laugh perhaps? We dived about a 100ft and the G-force went straight to my head. Then the Pilot's voice come over on the tannoy and said, "We have been fired at, but have deployed a stream of hot chaff as a counter-measure". This explained the fireworks I had seen. Hot chaff is hot metal they fire away from the plane so heat-seeking missiles follow the metal and not the plane (I learnt that back in Wales luckily). I calmed down, and was now in a hyper-vigilant state, a state I think I remained in until I left Kuwait six weeks later on my first 'R&R break'. When you are faced with what seems like certain death it is amazing how you come to accept it. I just knew there was nothing I could do about it.

So continuing my adventure into Iraq, we eventually landed in Basra Air Station, I spent the night there in a Pod and then the next night I boarded a helicopter bound for Basra Palace. This was a former Palace of Saddam Hussein where the British, American and Dutch Consulates were located alongside their respective military bases. We flew with the back ramp open to the elements, with two gunners precariously positioned so they could shoot anyone wanting to shoot us. We flew low and fast, again the hot chaff was fired, which although it meant we were being fired at, I actually found it quite reassuring as it meant we hadn't been caught off guard.

I enjoyed the first helicopter ride into the compound,

and now felt ready for my six month money-making adventure in Iraq. I told myself if I died, I died, it was one of those things. I didn't realise how bad things would get, or how a future helicopter journey would become my number two on my list of life changing experiences.

I actually really enjoyed my time in Iraq and learnt many lessons about life. It taught me the importance of living when the threat of dying is so very real and in your face. I made some great friends, including "The Major" who I have already mentioned, my comrade and fellow Champagne lover Alexander who is the epitome of professionalism, and fun loving, young at heart Baroness Botha – my fantastic boss who was also into Yoga and Tai Chi. Most of us never left the compound, unless of course it was by helicopter, so we only glimpsed Basra City as we arrived and departed Basra Palace.

We were surrounded by a huge wall and protected by brave Gurkha guards and the military; it was very much like a prison on reflection. I adapted to life at Basra Prison, I mean Palace, quite quickly and things started to become "normal". We had a bar, a swimming pool, gym, golf buggy's to transport us to various shops and other parts of the compound, and we made the most of what we had. The rockets would usually come at night so we were relatively safe during the daytime. Every night we would hear the rocket alarm and depending on our location we would have to stay put inside a protected building, dive to the floor, or run to another building. I was never caught outside during a rocket attack so usually stayed in the bar or in my pod, depending on the day of the week. For months and months they failed to hit any buildings, only empty areas of dirt, then suddenly their accuracy improved. They hit one of the Pods belonging to the cooks. It went straight through his Pod and into another killing him almost instantly. Things looked serious, and the decision that only essential personnel should remain was taken, so muggins here volunteered to stay. The selfish buggers outside the walls began to rocket us during daylight hours, which meant no more pool and tanning time for me – morale was at an all time low.

We stayed in Iraq for 6-7 weeks at a time then had to take a week holiday to decompress from the stressful environment. After six weeks eating, socialising and working with the same people and living in a state of hyper-vigilance you need the break, trust me. I decided to go to Australia and visit Thom's Brother (and my friend) Dan, who was traveling there during the summer.

We had so many rocket attacks on the run up to my helicopter flight that I kept getting bumped off so more troops could move around Basra. For the third time that week I had a new helicopter flight scheduled, this time for Saturday 6 May (2006) but again was bumped off for someone from the military. I was getting so annoyed and just wanted to leave and go on my well-deserved holiday. But on this occasion the cancellation put things into perspective for me, that 3rd helicopter I was due to board was shot down over Basra city before it ever reached the Palace compound. All five souls on board sadly died. I was no longer so keen to leave for Australia.

Wes had seen the news in the UK and knew I was due out on a helicopter that day, he tried ringing my UK and Iraqi mobile with no luck, and couldn't reach me on emails as we were all sheltered in the basement of the Consulate-General under 'lock-down'. That meant no incoming or outgoing phone calls to avoid security leaks and interception by the insurgents. When I finally got back to my pod I called Wes and he was fuming, he was in tears and told me he thought I had gone down and been killed in the helicopter. I explained the situation and he understood.

I safely flew out the next evening, via Bahrain and eventually got to Australia. I had a great time, and only on the way back to Basra did the full weight of what had previously happened hit me. It changed my life forever, and made me so grateful to be alive. I also realised how selfish I had been by going to Iraq when I had so many people back home who loved me. I stayed until October, eight months in total. The final straw for me was when I was sitting in my pod and I heard an explosion so loud that I thought a rocket had landed outside my front door. I calmly slipped down my sofa as if my skeleton was made of jelly and crawled to the 'safety' of my bathroom. I sat on the floor in my body armour for 30 minutes and decided enough was enough, sod the money I am out of here! I departed the next month. My heart goes out to the troops who are unable to take that decision.

The situation rapidly deteriorated and eventually the UK withdrew to the Airbase as things at Basra Palace were too dodgy. It put many things into perspective and without sounding like a mercenary it paid off all my debts. I have so many surreal and funny stories from that time, and it made me realise that death is not something to be scared of, it encourages us to live our lives fully. Iraq changed my life, in fact it gave me a new lease of life, and it helped me to see things differently. I have never felt so alive and that was probably because death was so close.

I am certainly not frightened of death anymore, I am scared that I won't have done everything I want to before dying, but that attitude pushes me towards achieving my desires and goals and makes me relish every moment. By being mentally prepared for your own death I think we have a deeper understanding of the cycle of life, which helps you deal with death in a more objective manner.

I spent some time thinking about death, as one does in a war zone, and came up with the simple conclusion that it is the exact opposite of birth. I know that sounds simple, but it is. I know that death will strike me at an unexpected time, hopefully not until I am old, and it is something I don't have any control over. Medical advances, exercise, and a good diet can help to some degree but I think when our time is up, it's up. I think we all have some kind of sell-by-date! Once we have achieved what we are here to do, or perhaps once we have given up on living life, our time will come to an end. I don't think we go into an afterlife as such. No heaven, no hell, and no purgatory. Just to the earth in full form, or in ashes. From there we get absorbed into the soil, turned into nutrients and minerals and then perhaps get eaten by an animal at the lower end of the food chain and the whole process begins again in one great circle of life – "The Lion King" couldn't have put it better really.

I do think to some degree that our legacy (our consciousness) lives on. By sharing our knowledge and wisdom with others, our flow of consciousness (soul or

Spirit) gets carried forward to the next generation, or this happens by some other greater force. I also have this feeling that some part of us goes to another plane of existence, the infinite capacity of space, or somewhere unexplained, and is unlikely ever to be discovered through all of mankind's existence. I have already touched on reincarnation in Part 1 of the Karma Lost Key, and that helps me answer many questions about the issue of life after death. I find it a mystery waiting to be discovered, but I don't think science will ever uncover those mysteries. The answers are to be found by us as we travel along our individual spiritual paths.

I was pondering on this when I was in the inner chamber of the Great Pyramid of Giza in Egypt. I was visiting Cairo as part of David Miliband's delegation when he was the Foreign Secretary. We were lucky enough to be given a private tour of the pyramid site one evening. As we climbed up the external side of this ancient structure towards a small opening I was amazed at the sheer scale of the thing. Although speculation still continues, effectively it was a tomb for royalty, and yet it has stood the test of time for 4000 plus years! As we all filed our way inside to a very small passageway I began to use my imagination and take myself back to the time of the Pharaohs.

The ceiling height was only about 3ft in places which was really hard work for someone like me at 6ft 3, still dressed in my suit and work shoes, but we eventually made it to the very top where the inner chamber was located. The whole time I was carrying the Foreign Secretary's Red Ministerial Box (lead lined and very heavy) as it contained some classified papers that I couldn't leave in the car. Our guide was telling us about how scientists thought it had been built, but I was in another time and place and I can't remember anything he said. I felt a deep routed connection to that place in Cairo, and I believe it has many more secrets to reveal in the future. It was fascinating to think that the structure I was slowly ascending was supposedly built for the sole purpose of ensuring the inhabitants reached the afterlife, something that the Egyptians were certain of. I snapped out of my daydream when I heard David Miliband laughing loudly and looking at me. He thought it was hilarious that I had brought the Red Box into the Pyramids, and said I must be very dedicated to the job!

That is one example of an ancient civilisation's attempt at uncovering the mysteries of life after death. Many more civilisations, generations, and religions have followed a similar quest for answers. Some believe they had found the answers, and most religions teach that a life of good deeds results in some sort of paradise or afterlife. This belief frightened people into behaving correctly and by doing so created an orderly society. **Paradise or heaven, whatever you want to call it, is here**. You are living it, **right now** – that is another well-kept secret of the Universe! Why wait for an afterlife that few people are sure about? It's all about our perception. Both Heaven and Hell are in this very world, they are in our mind. We choose what we want to see and experience.

As death is as certain as birth there is no time like the present to live a life in paradise and make the most of everything we have. Live each day as if it is your last, bearing in mind that your actions have consequences, and you will begin to fully appreciate the Heaven in which we are living right now.

The fourth thing on my list that changed my whole direction in life was the death of my older sister Vicki. She sadly died soon after my Granddad. Vicki was unfortunate to have had several life threatening illnesses throughout her lifetime – she was ill enough for all of us, but I suppose I had expected her to pull through like she had always done in the past. She was a born fighter, and a feisty cow.

I had visited her in hospital before leaving the UK to visit Laura (my other sis) and her boyfriend Steve in Australia, and I remember walking away from Vicki and it felt strangely different to other goodbyes. I turned around to wave goodbye to her, and as she stood there next to her hospital bed I saw her differently, she seemed innocent and child like, at peace almost, and she had a few tears in her eyes. I think she knew it would be the last time she would see her younger brother. As I look back now I can remember just seeing her and not much of the ward or other people, it was like tunnel vision.

As Steve, Laura and I were driving down the East Coast of Oz we got a call from my Mum saying that Vicki had died in the early hours of Monday morning. We pulled over to a lay-by in the middle of nowhere and started making calls to Airlines and the Insurance Companies. It wasn't a total shock, as we knew she was seriously ill, but it was an awful feeling. Steve was so good during our frantic scramble back to England. I don't know if we could have done it without him. He sorted tickets, refunds, and transfers, and was a great source of comfort for both of us during our four day trip back around the world. We had to stay overnight in Tokyo airport, and none of us had slept very well for days. Fanny (Laura's rather unfortunate nickname) couldn't get comfortable on the airport seats and was close to tears through exhaustion and the sad news, so Steve made a bed for her on the floor with various things from his backpack. She slept peacefully as I lay awake staring at the ceiling wondering how all of this would change and affect us as a family. On the return flight to London from Tokyo we were split up due to the last minute arrangements. I decided to watch a film called "PS I Love You" without knowing anything about the storyline – I soon realised it wasn't such a great choice. So not for the first time, and by no means the last time in my life, I found myself crying 30000ft in the air surrounded by perfect strangers.

I don't know what it is with planes, but I always find myself thinking deeply on them, maybe it's because it is a sort of no-mans land and I feel I can shut out the world and its distractions. Through work I've been on more Private Jets than I have budget airlines, and hired entire planes and even kept a 747 waiting for 30 minutes while I located some missing luggage, but each one of my many journeys has always brought out the thinker in me. Just a shame I wasn't seated next to Fanny and Steve when I needed familiar faces the most on that return journey from Australia.

I previously wrote that I wasn't sure how I would react to another young death now I was more spiritually aware. I wasn't sure if I was ok with my Granddad's death because he was old, or because I was in touch with my spirituality. Now, I didn't have a choice, my spiritual beliefs were going to be tested. I was so upset to hear that she was gone, and it didn't really hit home for ages, but during her most recent period of illness I knew there would be one of two outcomes. She would either fight at another chance at life and turn her attitude and thinking around, or she would decide to give up and call it a day. That may sound emotionless, but I knew she had given up the fight this time around, and was ready to rest, and she can't be blamed for that.

I think she was finished with life on this plain, she was finished with hurt in both physical and emotional terms, and she was finished with **her world**. On another level there were so many lessons that everyone who knew her will learn from, it's just sad that they will only see these lessons after she is gone.

She died at the age of twenty-nine, my sister Vicki who I imagined meeting for drinks when I was in my 40s; talking about her kids, and laughing about years gone by. She was always so happy, fun, and loved to wind us up, her laughter would fill the house. She is now gone forever and as hard as that is to accept, I know there is absolutely sod all I can do about it. There is also nothing I can do to have one last dance with her, share another laugh or tell her once more "that I love who you are", and I can't turn back the clock and tell her "don't worry about the times you were nasty to me".

It must be so easy to play all this over in your mind and ask yourself "why didn't I say that or do this" but we have to realise we can do nothing to change the past and the 'what if' game never works. So I move forward with *my life,* **and** *learn from hers*. I live life, I really do. This is my heaven right now, on earth. I love every second of life, as I know it could all vanish, just like that.

Vicki still lives on in our memories, and her death is something I have to accept or let it consume me. Her time was up, I hope she learnt the lessons her Spirit had intended for her, and that her Spirit returns in an easier embodiment next time around.

I choose to live my life where hers stopped so suddenly, live it like each breath is my last, because life really is too short not to live each moment in the 'now'. I owe it to her to live my life fully.

To anyone experiencing the death of a loved one, it does become easier with time, it has too. The empty hole can never be filled but you can learn to live without them. Memories are powerful things and they are important, they are a way of keeping the deceased alive. It is funny to think we only tend to remember the good in people when they are gone; perhaps a reminder for each of us to do more good in the world. Regardless of their age, it helps to remember the happiness they experienced, and the life they lived. Accept the hand of fate as best you can, don't blame God, others, or yourself. Just like a candle in the wind, we can never be sure when life will be extinguished. It is the gamble we all pay when we play the game of life.

I find myself unexpectedly dedicating this Lost Key to Vicki, my cheeky, feisty, fun, caring, dancing, honest, sensitive, and loving older sister. I miss you so much Vicks, but 'Notorious Victorious' you know you are not easily forgotten!

Xxx

14
Part 1

No Such Thing as an Illness – The Power of The Mind

♪ Feeling Good, Nina Simone ♪

I HAVE NEVER BEEN REALLY ILL, which I am thankful for, but Vicki had more than her fair share. We joked that she had been ill enough for all of us put together. She had a rare blood condition when she was younger, called Diamond Blackfan Anaemia, which basically meant her bone marrow didn't make enough red blood cells. Then when she was about sixteen she suffered a brain haemorrhage, had two serious brain operations and almost died several times. In the years following she was diagnosed with loads of aneurisms and had a slight stroke. She more recently had breast cancer and then, probably due to the cocktail of drugs she had to take, we discovered she had cancer of the bone marrow, which eventually got the better of her.

There is a New Age thought that illness or disease affects us when we are not at ease with ourselves. I believe this and think it's the main cause for many illnesses. When I was doing Psychology at College I remember learning about experiments in which some of the participants were given sugar pills with no active ingredients, and others were given the medication being tested. Those participants who took the sugar pills mainly imitated the reactions of those who took the medication. What this showed was that if those participants thought and believed in something strongly enough, in their case the 'medication' (the sugar pill), it manifested into reality. This is called the placebo effect.

I thought this was amazing. Particularly because my Mum and her friends have always claimed that if you think positively and strongly enough then a thought will come true (I don't think the lottery counts though). The power of the mind still amazes me, and I feel we all hugely underestimate it. There is a scientific fact that states we only use something like a third of our brain. This still makes us the most intelligent beings on the planet, so imagine our potential if we used 100% of it! I am sure that day will come with much practice and time. I have a funny feeling that at least another third of our brain will be for spiritual or psychic use, for example telekinesis. But for now I think we can use the power of positive thought to help ourselves, in particular to change our state of health for the better.

There isn't a secret spell or potion that will produce eternal health for all who seek it. It is simply about combining the right mindset and lifestyle. You have to create a balance internally, and a balance with the external world to promote wellbeing within your body.

So what is the right mindset? Well it obviously involves spirituality otherwise I wouldn't be writing about it, but it's also about having a positive outlook. If you're always thinking, "I am ill, something is wrong with me" or "I know I will get cancer" then it is bound to manifest into reality. If on the other hand you don't let it cross your mind and think positively about your future and current state of health, it will also manifest into reality. Thinking positively about all sorts of things in your life, not only your health, will have a positive effect on your circumstances.

Our mind is the single biggest tool we have. I had an epiphany when I was in the shower the other week. I was washing my arms and I thought to myself my body is just made up of limbs and a torso. The real jewel, and the most important thing I own is my mind – it controls everything, not only my body, but the outside world as well. It controls how I see things, what I do day to day, what I think, what I say, what I believe, and everything in between. A positive mental attitude is the most important thing that helps make up a healthy person. But there are other factors, and that includes our lifestyle choices.

I have already talked about diet and its effects on happiness and wellbeing in a separate Lost Key.

Obviously, if you follow a poor diet with chemicals and additives it will eventually be reflected in your state of health. The healthier and more natural the food you eat, the healthier the outcome will be. Imagine a diet of fast-food every day of the week, washed down with bucket loads of fizzy drinks and cigarettes for good measure – I don't see that as a ticket to perfect health – do you? I hate to say it, but we also need to exercise. I despised sports at school and couldn't see the point of chasing a football around the field. you would often find Thom and I on the sidelines, gossiping, instead of running after the ball. That was before Thom somehow managed to get the Dr to write a note to say he was allergic to grass, the clever guy.

As we get older and are not forced to do sports by teachers, we need to carry out some form of exercise. A healthy body contributes to a healthy mind, which in turn contributes to that thing we are all in search of ......happiness. That may seem hard to believe when exercise is painful, but it is sadly true. Just find something you can learn to enjoy, whether that's pushing yourself at the gym, yoga, pilates, swimming, tennis or simply walking more. Do something that uses our amazing gift – the body. Make it a routine as our minds sometimes find familiarity easier to cope with. I personally find running and yoga a great way of relaxing, but any type of exercise promotes a happy and healthy mind and body. These ideas are not new or necessarily spiritual but they have been proven by government health advisers and scientists the world over.

On top of these obvious lifestyle choices, I think

that illnesses are reflected in certain personality types more than others. Those people who are always stressed, living on the edge, and are always having emotional ups and downs are far more prone to illness than those who are more relaxed. So chilling out once in a while will keep your body in tip top condition, why not use some of the techniques I outlined in the "Chilling & Zoning Out" Lost Key?

This might seem a bit outrageous to people who are ill, or people who know others who are ill, but try to think about it logically and objectively. I strongly believe that having an illness is our body's way of telling us that something is wrong with our lifestyle, emotions, past experiences, or spirituality. An illness or disease is our body's way of screaming out to us saying, "hey, sort it out, this is wrong". The very word disease spells out <u>dis</u> – <u>ease</u>, i.e. not at ease. I feel that most illnesses are due to some form of internal imbalance. There are examples of external influences that can cause illness such as cigarettes, alcohol and drug abuse etc, but by the same token they can be attributed to our internal imbalance.

Take severe alcohol induced illness – the illness is created from drinking too much, but the reason the person drinks too much in the first place is due to some kind of internal imbalance. Perhaps lack of self-esteem, stemming from a deep routed problem in childhood no doubt. No imbalance, no illness, simple as that.

Past experiences that have not been dealt with are the biggest contributing factors to illness. They fester in our minds and eat away at us provoking the onset of ill health. Most of our illnesses are now treated with some kind of man-made drug, but some illnesses will never go away unless you learn to deal with your underlying problems. This is why I made past experiences the first chapter of The Lost Keys. It is the starting point to a happier, healthier and more spiritual life.

At the moment, I don't think we are aware enough of our own capabilities. In the future I believe that illnesses will vanish as we learn to deal with our imbalances. Medicine as we know it will have a different place in the new age day-to-day life. For now, medicine serves a purpose, but bear in mind that the results could be down to the placebo effect. It has unquestionably saved the lives of countless people, including my family and friends. However, from my experience it doesn't actually uncover and treat the root cause of the problem, it just finds a way of covering it up and curing it. Some people would say "So what, it cures it, how can you complain?" but it's like putting sticky tape over a crack in a dam, it will only hold for so long!

We will get there without a doubt, but for now most of us will have to rely on modern medicine for the worst illnesses and diseases, but do try thinking positively about your state of health, or simply try not thinking negatively, and I am sure it will make a big difference.

Just as catalyst to promote everyone's desire to try and 'self heal', think about what you are actually taking in order to "get better". Prozac in order to make you happy and Paracetamol to cure headaches! Pills to make you happy just seems like science fiction to me, why not just take pills to make you smile, laugh, love and be done with emotions altogether?! Headaches are almost always 90% from dehydration or poor diet. Why rely on an external source when you can cure it yourself?

For people who suffer from things like smoking induced cancers they need to ask themselves why they continued to smoke when they knew the dangers. They can blame the addictive substances contained in fags, but at the end of the day they had the **ability** to stop something they knew was bad for them. All it takes is for their **motivation** to be strong enough. A smoker will only give up smoking when they want to. We all have a responsibility to look after our bodies, and have the power to influence or change everything that occurs around us.

Illness and disease doesn't just stem from negative thinking or not being at ease with yourself. It could also be a way of teaching us a big life lesson, or repaying some Karma. But you can help yourself by thinking positively and changing certain things.

Mental health also plays a big part in our society, especially in the Western world. If you find yourself feeling low or depressed, ask yourself why you are feeling like that? Analyse and spend time on "you", learn about yourself and find out what makes you happy and unhappy. If you are unhappy, there is a good reason for it. Maybe you are on the wrong path and your spirit is trying to tell you to move on, maybe you aren't comfortable with who you are, maybe you don't know who you are, maybe you expect too much from others and need to focus more on yourself.

If you are feeling depressed or unhappy it is because

you are not living your life as you should be. **It is the Universe's way of slapping you in the face to help you make some positive changes.** It may seem as if you are in a dark hole and can't escape, but there is light at the end of the tunnel, I promise you that. When depressed or in a dark place try not to dwell or think too much, try to hold onto the positives in your life, and search for the hidden meaning and lessons you need to learn.

I was in that place many years ago when I was first starting out on my spiritual journey so I know what it is like. By experiencing depression it gave me the kick I needed to achieve my destiny, and put me back on the right path. Just know you will get through it, however long it *needs* to take, and remember the positives. Have faith. Ask for signs, and you will be helped.

We are all guilty of getting wrapped up in the unimportant pre-occupations surrounding us, but sometimes you just need to take a step back from all of it and evaluate yourself and your life choices. Although I say spend time on yourself, and without wanting to sound contradictory, when I was feeling depressed I found it was because I was over-analysing and questioning things *too* much. So be careful not to get consumed by yourself. **Don't think too much**, just enough to be aware of you, and life around you. Wesley was a prime example of this, he would think so much about everything that I could see he was becoming consumed by it, and he wasn't actually living in the now. He was just like a stuck record, mulling over all the situations that had occurred or had not yet happened. "What is the point?" I would ask him, "You won't achieve anything from going round in circles". I told him he thought too much, and needed to live more in the present. I think we could all do with remembering that. Your mind is the most powerful tool you will ever own so use it wisely and don't be 'diseased', be at 'ease'.

14
Part 2

The Power of The Mind – Mind Over Matter

♪ *World's Greatest, R Kelly* ♪

THE POWER OF THE MIND can influence who we meet, social situations, our outlook on life, future events that are yet to happen, our health, circumstances we find ourselves in, emotions, and virtually everything physical or otherwise.

The monotheistic religions (Christianity, Islam etc) look for miracles or interaction from some form of higher power, but we have that capability within us. **Within every single one of us**. The key is to tap into that strength, and truly believe in the power within. I believe that such focused thought is used when praying, that any results are solely attributable to the power of the mind, not a God in heaven somewhere in the clouds. If praying works then fine, but it is unnecessary to look skywards for such miracles.

At the moment the power of the mind is revealing itself regularly. Take a recent Christmas as a prime example; I felt I really wanted to meet someone exactly like me. A week later I met someone who was so similar that we repelled each other like two positive ends of a magnet! This person shared virtually every personality trait I have. However, after spending some time with that particular person I realised they were not what I needed after all, and from that encounter I learnt to value the differences in peoples personalities. 'Like for like' isn't always a good thing. That is a great example of using my power within to find such a person, and then using my ability to learn from what could have otherwise been seen as a negative experience. This is the New Age thinking in perfect play!! What we **want** isn't always what we **need.**

Another example is when I am thinking about a particular issue I don't understand, I find myself meeting someone the next day who happens to bring it up in conversation. Or a book will jump out at me in a bookshop or from my own collection that contains the very information I wanted to uncover. Not literally jump into my hands – I am no sorcerer, but it somehow stands out, or my eyes are drawn to it. On Valentines Day not so long ago I was wondering if a certain someone from work thought of me as more than a friend. I suppose I asked myself or the Universe for a sign, trusted I would receive one in good time, and later that day, much to my embarrassment, I had a present appear on my desk!

It's so amazing when you start to see all of this unfold around you. It's like my mind, or perhaps my higher mind is sending out these questions into the world and then I receive the answers in the form of real life situations. Sometimes it just blows me away.

I now find myself thinking about the consequence of every thought I have. At first this was a curse, and hard work, but then as the positive things I thought about or questioned materialised, I realised it could only be a good thing in the long run and keeps my thoughts positive.

I am aware of every tiny thought that I conjure up. I can't really put this new awareness into words, I guess it feels natural now and makes me wonder what the hell I was doing before! Trust me though, it is life changing and gives a sense of control over the world, not in a dominating power-hungry way, but in a way that makes you feel part of the wider picture and yet satisfying because you are taking responsibility for your life. I am now aware that I have something so much more inside me than organs, blood, and thought processes. We all do, and I think we always have. We just need to learn to open up and accept it.

Try it out – ask yourself (say it aloud or in your head) a question, or ask for something you need. Truly believe that the answer or result will drop into your lap when it is ready to do so. Have faith and trust that you will find what you seek. Then go about your business and think no more about it.

The mind works better and more in line with your true self if it can relax, so meditation and quiet moments free from distraction will help train it. When I need direction in my life or I am unsure of my next move in life I go to my bedroom, close the door, turn everything off and still my mind. I call it a **life review**. I then ask a question, usually "what am I supposed to be doing with my life" or "what is my purpose" I wait, relax and see what comes up. The same thing has come back each time for the last seven years – "write a modern New Age book for the NetGen".

Don't force an answer and don't just fantasise, rest in a state of openness. You might get a message, a thought, or an idea, or you might get sod all. It will come when you are ready to hear it, in a way you will understand. Don't expect or force your mind. For me, answers started coming to me when I meditated, then I started seeing messages in normal things like books and nature, and now the answers mostly appear as fully formed ideas at the same moment I ask the question. I have to reach for a pen as it appears so quickly and comes with much detail.

To me none of this is strange or new, Mum had always taught us that the power of the mind was very important and positive thinking was key. As we grew up if we ever voiced negativity or said "I can't", she would always say "there is no such thing as can't" and quote two words at us "positive thinking". I suppose for the people who didn't have similar lessons drummed into them as youths it can seem slightly odd. I liken it to throwing and catching a ball. When a ball is thrown at you, you tell your mind to catch it, and you usually do catch it. By thinking positively about something that is yet to happen you are gearing yourself up to achieving it. Give your mind a bit more credit and begin to watch your thoughts.

Translate the real truth behind that saying in the bible **"Ask and you shall receive!"**

15

Wise Up To The Real Reality – Putting Things Into Perspective

♪ *Do They Know Its Christmas, Band Aid* ♪

We, as Westerners, have so much activity surrounding us and are always busy with something. Over the years I have realised it is very important not to get caught up with these distractions. It is far too easy to lose sight of the meaning of life and ignore the important signs and experiences that change us for the better. I find a great way to stay balanced is to put my life into perspective and open my eyes to the less fortunate people who battle to stay alive everyday.

My jobs have involved much travelling and I often

spend the majority of that time by myself, so I use it for contemplation. I went to Bangladesh on a two-day trip and whilst there I was thinking how tired I was and that I wanted to be back in London, in my lovely flat with Jen overlooking the big city. As soon as I had thought this, I began to analyse my thoughts and asked myself why I wasn't content being where I was in that particular moment of time.

I started gazing out the window of my 5 star hotel and from my room on the 18th floor I saw Dhaka (the capital) for what it really was. I looked carefully at the people who appeared to be like ants going about their daily life. I saw people selling fruit from a cart attached to their bike. Kids were playing in rubbish heaps – or so I thought – looking closer I realised they were actually scavenging through the rubbish for food or bits they could re-use. People were using the streets as public toilets, men lifting their loin clothes and crapping in full view. There were whole families crammed into toy-sized taxis, with their huge baskets and luggage strapped precariously to the roof. Looking across the smoggy city I could see the rooftops were dotted with fabric that acted as tent-like shelters, and then I saw an elderly woman emerge from one with her washing. She spent about an hour washing and scrubbing three saris.

I was absorbing all of this for at least three hours, and it really touched me on a level I had never experienced before. The only thing that appeared to live with relative ease in this place were the Eagles that were circling over a slum area positioned straight ahead of me. I started to cry once I had taken stock of the scene spread out in front of me, framed by my huge glass window. I was crying because I was filled with sympathy and empathy for the poor unfortunate people that I could see in every direction. I felt so sorry for them but at the same time I felt grateful that I hadn't been born into such an existence. These people – children, adults, elderly and disabled were suffering immensely every single day, and there was I, worried about getting back to my flat in London! I told myself how bloody selfish and stupid I was, when scenes like this were happening every day, every hour, and every minute throughout the world. It put so many things into perspective.

A car came to pick me up from the hotel that afternoon, and on the journey through the city I could see the expressions of pain etched onto the faces of the locals. Kids jumped up at the windows and begged me for money with tears streaming down their malnourished cheeks, grown men with missing limbs were lying in the street with a single cardboard sign in their hands and a glimmer of hope in their eyes, and elderly people were carrying huge amounts of logs on their backs with no shoes on their already worn-out feet. The kids and adults who were banging on my car window were literally starving to death. I had to fight back the tears as it was all too much to accept. The conditions that these people suffer are shocking, and when you see it first hand it is very upsetting and painful to accept the dramatic divides between the rich and poor. In contrast to my feelings and observations, one of my colleagues on the trip was debating which pearl necklace to buy, and that was all she seemed to care about – the nicest necklace, at the cheapest possible price!

We all think we have problems, we think we have issues, hard lives, bad luck, but no matter what we are going through in our own life, there will always be someone who is suffering considerably more, somewhere in the world.

We in the western world should be grateful for what we do have, our problems are **nothing**, absolutely **nothing** in comparison to so many others in the world. If you can afford it, take a trip to a third world country and see it first hand, your life will be changed forever, unless you are the Tin Man and you don't have a heart! If you can't afford to travel then watch some documentaries. These people are human and they are just like you and I. Educate yourself about the massive differences in our world and it will inadvertently help you realise you have nothing to complain or be upset about any longer, and will hopefully encourage more people to try and help in some practical way.

Think yourself lucky to have a commute to work – no matter how tough, you have a job to go to and have an income that supports you. So many people I know dwell on the things they don't have, or get upset because they want more. That could be more time, more love, more money, more anything. I look at what I **do** have, and all the good things in my life, and for me it is quite tiring to hear people moan about their life when they actually have so very much.

We all think we have issues, psychologically or otherwise, and dwell on them, get absorbed by them, and lose sight of the blessings we actually have. **Change your mindset and you change your outlook.**

While I was on my soul-searching trip to India I used my time to have a really detailed life review, which I mentioned earlier. It is something I aim to do twice a year. I set aside some time with no distractions, and look at where I have come from, where I am, and where I am going. I focus on what is important to me, and look at the plans I have for the future. I used to spend more time planning a night out than I did planning my life – quite scary really. At the rate at which time is slipping away from us I think it is really important to keep track of our individual journeys. By giving yourself a life review you are able to effectively stop time, take stock and change direction – if a change is what is required. Listen to your mind and you won't go wrong. It is also a great way to put things into perspective.

It really upsets me when I hear people complaining about problems that are 99% of the time inconsequential, like "I am bored" or "I am feeling really depressed or anxious" or "the cashier really annoyed me when.." Granted, the person thinking about their problems really believes that their issues are important or insurmountable. However, if you put them into perspective you will begin to see that your life is a gift that should be spent on more important actions and thoughts. Just change your mindset, and if all you can do is think of people less fortunate each time, I am certain it will adjust our ridiculous western, self obsessed, self centred, materialistic attitudes. Next time you are 'bored', take the time to think about people in Africa, for example, who are starving, who are homeless, who are crying out in pain, lying in the scorching sun asking "why us, why so much pain and unfairness?" We could all do with getting our heads out of the sand.

I saw the direct opposite of my experience in Bangladesh when I went to Chelsea (London). I helped a family friend clean the carpet of her flat that she rents out. She can't walk very well or bend down and as I lived just around the corner my Mum volunteered my services and I was happy to oblige. After I finished the job she took me to a cafe on Kings Road (one of the most expensive roads for property and retail in the UK) and we sat outside and watched the world go by. As I was sitting there absorbing the comforts of this affluent area, I realised how easy it was to get caught up in the material world. Kings Road advertises an easy, carefree, everything's rosy type of lifestyle. The people I saw only seemed to care about how they looked in their designer gear and about getting as much shopping done as possible. I could see how they could get preoccupied with this type of lifestyle when it blocks out a lot of the mundane things in life. It doesn't allow much time for thinking about the meaning of life, or the deeper more important questions we all ask at some stage!

I don't think preoccupying ourselves with shopping and material activities brings happiness though. You can meet the happiest dustman and the most suicidal of city bankers. Some of the happiest people in the world are those on middle incomes and content with their lot in life. Whoever invented the saying that money can't buy happiness was wise beyond their years. Money can never buy you happiness, as happiness cannot be found through external means. Happiness can only be found and developed internally. I suppose if you won the lottery tomorrow it would bring temporary happiness, and I suppose it would make for an easier life but the more we have, the more it complicates matters as we then fear losing it!

I know the people I saw on Kings Road on that Sunday live a very privileged life, but a large majority of affluent people are usually emotionally unstable and unhappy, and the most under-privileged when it comes to having a strong state of mind. They base their happiness around the money they have, or the highs they can experience from using that money. Money fluctuates and is a very fickle thing. If you have it, you either constantly want more, or are concerned that it will run out. I am sure if you asked yourself honestly what the secret to happiness is, the answer would never be money.

When the preoccupations those Chelsea folk fill their lives with stops for a tiny moment, they, like everyone else realise that there is something missing that cannot be filled with money, or by keeping themselves busy with material distractions or activities. <u>That missing something</u> (the original name for this book) is unquestionably **Spirituality**.

After re-reading my comparisons between the rich Chelsea people and the poor Bangladeshis, it shocked me to realise that the differences between the west and third world countries are so massive. It almost seems to me that the world and all the boundaries we humans have labelled "countries" are in need of a total rebalancing.

A rebalancing of wealth, resources, and spiritual teachings.

What I hope we are all destined for is a world where our needs are taken care of as they are in the Western world (for example toilets and clean water), but where we have a greater respect for the important things in life, things that really matter; like our personal development and spirituality.

Through our *material* evolution our lives have become easier in some ways, but scientific/ technological inventions and discoveries have not answered or helped with the question that so many people were asking even back in Egyptian times – **the question of our very purpose for being here, and our reason for living.** We have barely even scratched the surface when it comes to our *spiritual* evolution and development.

The East on the other hand has experienced the opposite of this. They have followed the spiritual path since the philosophical teachings of Buddha were first taught over two thousands years ago. The people of these countries have grown mentally and spiritually beyond anything comparable in the West. They have evolved and developed internally but their external world has stayed relatively unchanged. These people generally live in what we would call poverty, but I am sure they would say that we live in poverty, **poverty of the mind**! Something I am sure they would consider far worse than poverty in the material sense.

I went to Nepal by myself on a four-day break after I had finished working in Iraq, a sort of rest and relaxation holiday for myself. I was staying in a stunning hotel in the middle of a lake in Pokhara (a region outside the Capital city). One evening the local bartender told me about an amazing sunrise that could be seen from the top of the tallest hill in the valley. That same evening I arranged for a guide to meet me and take me to the summit the next day. Four-thirty a.m. arrived too quickly! I layered up, boarded the floating rope bridge to get to the shore, met my guide and got into his battered old car. As we got nearer to the summit I caught a glimpse of the sun rising over the snow-capped mountains that surrounded the valley of hills, lakes and lush forests.

On the way up I said to my guide how lucky they were to have such amazing views, tranquil settings, and an environment free from the modern hassles that I am subjected to on a day-to-day basis. He agreed with me and said that it made him thankful to live on such a beautiful planet, but he replied that it must be nice to have such comforts as electricity and clean running water. I felt terrible! My Aunt and Uncle have a picture hanging in their bathroom that has always made me stop and ponder, it reads, "The grass may be greener on the other side, but it's just as hard to cut." An apt saying I think.

Whether you are brought up in the western material world, or the eastern spiritual world, it appears to me there are good and bad points to both. **Its how we deal with the bad points that defines us, and sets us free from the possible causes of suffering.**

As I was travelling through Nepal and observing some of the poorest people I had ever seen, I couldn't help but notice their natural facial expressions were full of happiness, and all too often I would see them laughing at the small inconsequential things. They had an inner beauty and warmth that would quite literally shine through their poor living conditions. They were not as close to the poverty line as the people I saw in Bangladesh, but their lifestyles were definitely horrific in comparison to the poorest people we would ever see in the UK.

One afternoon I took a rowing boat to the otherside of the lake so I could trek up a large hill to reach a World Peace Pagoda. I say 'took' a rowing boat – I was in fact rowed across the lake (this was a rest and relaxation holiday after all!). On my journey across the peaceful placid lake I saw a whole family washing at the shore. They were all laughing and playing, and even the adults who were washing the youngest of the family were smiling and had an unexplainable quality and light about them. Once I had reached the top of the hill after a long and tiresome trek, I took a few deep breaths and looked 360 degrees around me.

I couldn't help but think that all of our western priorities were wrong. As I sat down in front of the Pagoda and soaked up the atmosphere and the stunning panoramic scenery, I asked myself **what was more important than understanding who we are, and what we are here for**? I didn't take a watch on this trek as I didn't want to be affected by time constraints. Some time passed and I came to a conclusion that nothing was more important – by becoming more spiritually aware we could overcome absolutely any obstacles that were thrown at us. All we needed was some time for ourselves in our fast-paced ever-evolving world. Even one hour a week spent evaluating and looking inwardly would help, we just needed to **STOP** for a moment and meditate on our lives. I concluded that if the people I saw by the lake could be happy with their life, simply through the practice of Buddhism, then we in the West should be more than capable of filling our "voids" by taking a similar approach. Clearly our preoccupations with material evolution hadn't worked in the last 200 years so what the hell had we got to lose by trying the Eastern way of evolving, **evolving spiritually**?

We all need to wise up, there is much more happening in the world than in our little bubbles of existence. The world does not revolve around us and our dramas. There are bigger things happening, and people who are suffering in ways we cannot imagine. Next time you are bored, feeling blue, anxious or are annoyed at the cashier who wouldn't give you a refund then ask yourself if it really matters that much. Get a grip, give yourself a talking to, and instead of moaning and whingeing be grateful for what you do have.

We really have so much compared to the millions that literally have nothing. And if you don't like what you have then **do something** about it. Spend your energy creating positive change rather than negative thinking.

16

The Devil Within – Anger

♪ *Bust Your Windows, Jazmine Sullivan* ♪

ONE OF THE "SINS" MANY of us are guilty of is anger. My friends know that I don't, and have never acted in an aggressive manner. Wesley once said to me he thought it was because I had no emotions (the cheeky bugger), but I think that was because he couldn't understand why I had never shown or discussed anger, which he considered to be a normal emotion in everyone. When I was between eight and fifteen years old I suppose you could say I became 'angry' with Laura quite a lot as she would do things to intentionally wind me up (as brothers and sisters do) but that is about the only time I can ever recall getting angry and showing it. More often than not I would end up in floods of tears on the floor like I had just had a mental breakdown. I just found she had the ability to push me over the edge and ruin my internal balance.

Maybe it is because I grew up knowing that anger can only lead to bad actions because of my Dad's behaviour towards my Mum before they got divorced. Maybe it was because I grew up in an all female household. Or maybe I don't naturally possess that characteristic. Either way, I know what it is like not to feel anger and therefore have no need to show it.

Anger can be controlled very simply if you put your mind to it. There is no point trying to suppress angry feelings because they are likely to explode or eat away at you. In order to get rid of them you have to deal with them proactively and in a logical manner. You can only really approach this if you have exorcised all of your demons from past experiences as I talked about in the first Lost Key. This is because past experiences that stay with you in to adulthood become a source of pain, and this pain can manifest itself as anger or illness.

Once you have a clean slate to work with you can begin to deal with the times when you feel yourself becoming angry. If you feel anger brewing up, assess the feeling. Is it a healthy feeling? Is it promoting your happiness? Is it resolving the situation? Is it helping you? I imagine the answers to all of the above would be no!

So from there, we need to assess the initial thought that triggered this feeling of anger or hatred. Ask yourself why you are angry, why did you start feeling that first bit of anger that snowballed out of control as it so often does.

Take this extreme hypothetical example. Catherine walks in on her boyfriend having sex with another woman. She gets extremely angry with her boyfriend for cheating, and gets jealous and angry at the woman in the bed. She smashes and breaks picture frames, punches her boyfriend, and wants to pull the bitch's hair out. Most people would argue this is a perfectly natural human reaction, but let's take this feeling of anger back to its roots.

– Why is she angry? She is angry because her boyfriend was with someone else and not her. His actions were untruthful and she felt hurt and jealous. She is angry with the other woman because she was part of the betrayal.

Both of these feelings come from attachment to her boyfriend, which is what happens when two people fall in love. But instead of feeling anger, which achieves nothing, she could turn this feeling into something productive that actually gets results. Instead of being angry, she could assess the situation in her own mind.

– Why is he cheating? Is it his fault, or hers? Does she want to be with someone who cannot fully commit? Is he the weaker one for cheating, or is Catherine for not knowing about it?

Through evaluating the situation calmly and logically Catherine can reach a clearer view, while maintaining a balanced mental state. In this case her boyfriend's insecurities are his problems, even though he has allowed them to affect Catherine. If they are *his* problems, what can Catherine do about it? Not much. And knowing this, believing this, she will realise that her anger is wasted on the situation and by staying focused and balanced in her actions she will come away from the situation with more control and less pain.

This method of breaking down anger is far easier to practice once you have started on the spiritual path and unlocked some of the other doors to happiness. Ultimately all anger can be broken down bit by bit until you reach a more positive emotion. Just go back to the first thought that sparked the feeling of anger and '**un-build**' it from there, usually it is a load of irrational rubbish and you are in fact to blame not the other person. Yes I did just say that! On some level, usually a deep level, we create every situation, so if something makes us angry, that something usually starts from within us. Most people get angry because they see their ego as being threatened and try to defend it, or because they cannot control a situation.

Anger is not a natural feeling; it is a feeling for those that do not have control over their emotions. Calmness and tranquillity are the personality traits of the spiritually aware, and is the state of mind that is achieved when you are aware of the universal truths and in touch with nature and yourself.

Anger can be seen in the eyes and in facial expressions. Look in a mirror and smile at it, really beam a smile at yourself and notice all of the feelings that come to mind (except for feeling an idiot!) and notice how your whole face looks, from any wrinkles to a glint in your eyes. Relax your face and now get angry, really angry, and stare in the mirror like you mean it. Notice the associated feelings and how you look. I find it amazing how our facial expression mirrors our emotions. They are quite literally written all over our face. I sometimes feel people must think I have escaped from a mental institute as I am always walking round with a grin on my face as I soak up every single detail of my day.

Someone else said to me recently that I don't appear to have any emotions, which I find really hard to swallow as I certainly have them, but only emotions that I consider as worthwhile. I wondered why it seems that I don't appear to have any, and I came to the conclusion that most people consider emotions like hatred, anger, and jealousy as emotions that make us human. I believe they make us **inhuman**. These negative emotions are massive sources of unhappiness because of the associated ups and downs we experience. I have a near perfect internal emotional balance because I have learnt to deal with emotions that have the potential to threaten my inner stability. It has become second nature to disregard small useless things such as anger. With this internal balance I have found a constant source of happiness and a kind of light within myself.

I urge everyone that sees negative emotions as part of us, to think of yourselves, and others, as higher forms of life that are beyond the pettiness and pointlessness of Neanderthal emotions. These unbalancing negative emotions lead to nothing but animosity, and pain. If a feeling brings pleasure without ill effects to others then I would class that as an emotion, anything else is simply unnecessary and needs readdressing or redirecting into something more positive and constructive.

The more I think about the New Age ideology, the

more I realise how quickly and enormously humans have evolved. The emotions that were once innate and instinctive are now outdated and redundant in our new world. Anger would have been useful when we needed to protect our caves and fight predators, but do we really need anger in the New Age?

Try and tame the devil within, even if you struggle at first to break down an angry thought, take a deep breath, count to ten, and ask yourself is it really worth the energy and stress of getting angry.

17

Underused Senses & Moving Forward – Senses & Our Future

♪ *I Believe*, Yolanda Adams ♪

*I*F WE COULD ONLY OPEN our eyes we would appreciate the true beauty of the planet we live on. And if we went about our daily lives and truly used all of our senses I believe it would transform our outlook for the better. We walk around this planet and see what we want to see, hear what we want to hear, and feel what we want to feel.

I am a good listener, and perhaps too much a listener and not much of a talker, but I know how important it is to use this sense. By listening to what people say, to truly listen to every word that comes out of their mouth you are becoming more at one with them. By intently listening you can see a person for what they are, you can see if they are uncomfortable in a situation, confident, happy, sad, amusing, deep, shallow, or truthful. You can pick up on so many aspects of a person's personality and nature just by listening to them without worrying what to say in reply.

It's so easy to be in a conversation and just think about what you are going to say next, how you might respond in order to look clever, or come across as something more than you are. Sometimes when I am talking to someone, even a close friend, you can see that they are itching to have their say and they almost completely ignore what I am saying. It's not only rude, but I think it's very self-centred and shows a lack of interest if nothing else. All it takes is to just slow the hell down.

The Monk in Burma who I stayed with for a day used to respond to my questions after a two-minute pause, a literal two minute pause which felt like an eternity when you are eagerly waiting for a response. At first I thought this was because he didn't understand my English but I soon realised he had no need to reply quickly, and by doing so the quality of his answers were incredible.

We all need to take a step back from this fast paced world, take a deep breath and slow down. Understand you will have your turn to input, disagree, respond or whatever; you don't need to worry about time suddenly running out! We all get swept up in this thing someone decided to call 'time', and it's our fear of this time running out that takes away the caring gentle side of our nature.

Jen (my old flatmate) and I had some fridge magnets in our flat that we inherited from our landlord. Each magnet had a different word on it. One evening I was standing looking into the fridge deciding what to concoct when I saw the word 'time'. Five minutes later I had made the following sentence "Is time a clever idea, or just an observation of self" – it just appeared. Now I haven't studied the meaning of this in any great detail, but it does strike me as interesting. If we had nothing to compare ourselves to, no trees, seasons, no age or youth, no day or night, then would time exist? If we couldn't compare ourselves to anything else and were just floating in the vacuum of space would time actually exist? Tricky tricky!

It is very easy to get caught up in the small details, but try and always have in the back of your mind that you are part of something **HUGE** and that you have time. You own time, time is at your disposal and not the other way around.

It worries me when I see people scramble for their phone, like their life depends on answering it. If I am out with friends or don't want to speak, I won't pick it up, my housemate Yuri is the same. The phone is there for MY convenience, not anyone else's. I lost eight phones one year, which was a record for me. But it really didn't bother me, the excess soon mounted up, but the actual 'not having a phone part' was a welcome relief. I think too many people see their phone, facebook, email, and internet as an extension of themselves. We need to be careful not to get consumed by these conveniences, they distract us from using our natural gifts of sight, smell, touch, hearing and taste. Instead of sitting on a bus checking facebook, why not look at your journey, hear what others are talking about, and feel what you are feeling in that moment.

Use the senses that you are lucky enough to possess – sight, hearing, touch, speech, and smell. Use them. Absorb everything, give your mind, body, and spirit as much detail as you can, and by doing so it will make you appreciate the complex design of this world. More importantly, start to use your sixth sense – psychic abilities.

Listen to those moments of intuition, follow them, have faith in their messages. Listen to your heart not your brain. If it feels right in your heart, follow that feeling. Start to follow your own sense of what is right or wrong, good or bad, and your future will unfold for you in the most positive way imaginable. We all experience magical psychic moments at some point in our life, we just choose to ignore them, or put them down to a 'coincidence'.

This filthy word, this *blasphemous* word makes me cringe every time I hear it, I think it should be banned from all dictionaries and languages. There is no such thing as a 'coincidence', "it is written" as the eloquent Arabs and Muslims say, or you or someone else has made it happen just by thinking it.

Those times when you are thinking about a friend and they phone you, or you bump into them in the street, or you pick up the phone and someone is already on the other end, or something that happens to me often – I was thinking about a particular person and while in a foreign country I bump into them! Imagine the chances of meeting one of your friends in another country, in another town, in another village, in a particular shop or a beach, at precisely the right time. The odds must be a trillion to one. If anyone ever says to me "that's just a big coincidence", I think they deserve a massive slap and someone needs to tell them to WAKE UP!!!!!!

For any of you disbelievers, take people like my Mum and her friends for example, who can read the past and future – there is no way they can know the information they relay. They are tapping into a knowledge that is available to all of us. I hope science does more to evaluate and prove the existence of the sixth sense, as some people won't believe in this ancient power until science has given it their rubber stamp of approval.

Why not have a psychic reading yourself to find out? All I ask is that you go with an open mind and don't put up a wall. You can see for yourself that the sixth sense really does exist. Some psychics are better than others, but no respected psychic will ever tell you when you are going to die, or other scary things. They will tell your past, present and applicable future.

I think we should all aim to cultivate our sixth sense as normally as we seek financial security. Take some quiet time, and close your eyes to listen to your inner voice, it will likely speak to you in the form of thoughts. The calmer and more spiritual you are from doing things like meditation (already outlined in the Meditating Lost Key) then the easier you can tap into your sixth sense. I think all schools should teach pupils to open and use their sixth sense in a dedicated lesson. Children find it so much easier than adults to develop psychic skills, as they haven't yet been conditioned with the world-view that only the physical can exist, and the future is unknown.

My Mum used to hold crystal-healing workshops in our adjoined barn when I was younger, and she taught a few specialised classes designed for my friends and I. These classes basically encouraged our creativity and opened our minds to other possibilities. We would draw our dreams and evaluate them, dowse in the garden, look at crystals and their various properties, perform basic healing on each other, and guess the pictures on concealed cards. We also imagined our perfect healing room complete with pills we could take if we ever became ill. It was great fun and kept us more engaged than when we were at school.

Who knows where our species might end up if we used our six senses to their full potential. I promise that even by using the five senses *properly* and more *consciously* you will begin to see the benefits. It is such a simple thing to do, and something most of us take for granted.

We humans are constantly evolving both in thought and with our technological advances. We are pushing forward as one species, making life better and easier with each new discovery. With this forward motion we can create amazing feats, or we can create havoc and come close to annihilating our existence on planet Earth, as Hiroshima and world wars have already demonstrated. We can all play a part in making this forward momentum something amazing, and something that our children, and their children's children can enjoy in peace and happiness.

We each make up part of our country and can make a huge difference by protesting peacefully or signing petitions. The situation in Tibet goes some way to highlight the power of individual intention. Tibetans have been oppressed by the Chinese dictatorship for far too long, and in March 2008 action was very slowly starting to take place. The mainly Buddhist Tibetans are a peaceful nation and don't believe in retaliating with violence. Until now the international community have ignored their problems because the country is of no real economic or geographical interest. This situation is also complicated by the fact that China has huge influence over western nations like our own. But thanks to the influence of individuals protesting, and independent journalists, international governments and organisations can no longer turn a blind eye to the genocide of Tibetan culture, people, and their religion. People around the world are calling for action and a call for action will eventually be heard. We are now capable of influencing the world by simply speaking up. The protests at the Beijing Olympics were a perfect example of individual action affecting a mass audience.

The few people in positions of power around the world who still hold onto their dictatorship with greed will vanish soon enough. Russia, China (hopefully sooner rather than later) the Middle East, and countries in Africa are all due for reorganisation at the top, and with each election, a new leader will be brought in, more in touch with their people and their spiritual instincts than the last. Heads of State around the globe will have a duty to be more answerable to their people. The USA is a prime example of this, having recently undergone a better change at the top. I think the world breathed a sigh of relief when George Bush got the boot from the White House!

The selfish action of individuals is due to stop very soon, there are far more people in the world who want love and peace than those who want war, power, fights and money. The selfish gain of territory and power is virtually behind us, we have learnt from history that it brings nothing but loss of life and unhappiness to millions of people and costs not only lives, but also loss of precious environmental resources.

The countries that are not lucky enough to have democracies will follow shortly behind us, and the world will be united with a common purpose; peaceful, harmonious human survival. We are literally standing at the **dawning of a New Age**.

I wrote the above in 2009, and as I read this back it makes me glad to see it's coming true. Especially if you take the 'Arab Spring' as a prime example, where it seemed everyone in the Middle East wanted change. Egypt and Libya in particular kicked out their Dictators and are in the process of becoming democracies. They may relapse, but they are currently taking steps in the right direction, and I hope all countries are destined for similar positive changes.

There is one thing that will change the human race forever and catapult our social and spiritual evolution forward at great speed – that is the discovery of a free, clean and renewable source of energy. When the time is right we will discover, or invent, a form of energy that will be free to everyone, ending the conflict and economic power struggles caused by worldwide fuel shortages. Perhaps it will come from an improvement in Nuclear physics, or utilise solar power in a more efficient way. I am hopeful that our clever scientists will step-up and transform everyone's life for the better.

We can now create temperatures hotter than the Sun! Imagine the reactions of scientists in the year 1700 if someone had suggested we were capable of such feats. This mind-blowing technology should be used for the good of mankind, not for destructive purposes and economic gain. This would not only help the third world develop, but it could also drive down the escalating costs in more developed nations and replace the dwindling oil supplies. This is what science should be working towards in our modern age; helping humanity live with more ease, at less cost, rather than giving us gadgets and technologies that we don't really need such as faster and smaller Iphones.

A cycle of the Mayan calendar ended on 21 December 2012 and many believed it would be the end of the world. In some ways they were right. I think it *was* the end of the world in a spiritual sense. It marked the end of the old way of seeing things, but at the same time it also marks the beginning of a new age of spiritual transformation. Most of my friends are currently embarking on some form of change, more inline with their individual truths, as am I, and we are doing it with less fear of failure and with more trust in our hearts. I welcome this new period with open arms because it can only improve our lives and that of others.

As more and more people awaken their special 'light'

within (a 'light' that stems from spirituality) it will send out a positive vibration invisible to the naked eye (like atoms and particles). A vibration so positive that it will cause dramatic shifts in both the physical and non-physical planes of existence. Without wanting to sound like a weirdo (I am probably too late to have that wish granted!), I liken it to a magic force field, sweeping and spreading throughout our world, touching all it passes with its immense transformative power. The more people that awaken, the more positive our planet and lives will become.

Much the same way you can feel good energy when you walk into a room full of happy people, imagine the feeling of the entire world being filled with good vibes! I hope I am around to see and feel that change in our world.

The biggest factor in moving forward as individuals is to let go of the past. **I can't stress that enough.** Sort it out. It is so important to rid ourselves of negative past experiences and if we can't do this, we will be like a stuck record and return to the same place we started from. Once we can do this, once we have learnt the lessons intended for us, we will have an untouched child-like quality, free of hang-ups and issues that will allow us to face the world and its contents with a clean psychological slate.

The world is our home, so let's make it a paradise we all want to be part of. Use your senses to help you be more present and aware, and realise that you are part of the spiritual evolution that is changing the world for the better.

18

The Unlocked Doors – Conclusion of The Lost Keys

♪ *Read All About It Part III, Emili Sande* ♪

MY SEARCH FOR HAPPINESS STARTED when I moved to 'The Big City' and found myself in a deep depression. I got lost in those dark thoughts and felt like there was no way out. When we hit rock bottom there is some conciliation that it can't get any worse, and the only way is up. I asked the Universe for help, and asked why it was happening to me. Two days later I rediscovered the New Age book my Mum had packed for me a month previously. It helped change my mindset, which I later realised was the source of all unhappiness. I questioned the purpose of life, and what **my** purpose was.

It's only now, after my long and winding journey on the spiritual path that I think I have an answer to that question. For what its worth, **I believe the purpose of life is to realise and achieve our dreams, learn the lessons that life throws at us, find true love, and be a kind, loving and generous person.** You will no doubt come up with your own versions but after much contemplation that was mine.

My vision at the moment is to run up and down an imaginary set of scales to maintain the balance, rather than sit in the middle. Not an orthodox image I know, but one that works best for me. At the weekend I love nothing more than spending time with my varied social groups, drinking, eating and having fun. During the week I meditate, practice Yoga, go running, use crystals, look inwardly and enjoy any form of interaction with nature that I can. The monk I met in Burma said I had reached a stage in my spiritual development that most people only begin to touch on during their middle age, if at all. My mindset has set me free, given me profound awareness of all things, and given me a constant source of happiness and a feeling of utter contentment and I am so thankful to everyone I have met who has guided me along this path.

Don't get me wrong I am *not perfect*, far from it, things still come up and I learn every day, but the lessons I learnt on my spiritual journey are engrained now. I can come back to them to find answers, support, and stability. I see things differently now, I am happy more than I am upset. If I can achieve all of these positive changes then I know everyone can. That is why I wrote this book, to share a cure for unhappiness.

The Lost Keys are the lessons I learned during my quest, but I think they are universal lessons that can help everyone deal with this world. **If you want to be happy you have to look at the world differently**, and I hope this book helps you do just that. Your journey is individual so learn what needs to be learnt, in your own time, in your own way.

You could change your world tomorrow, you could give up your job, follow your dreams, lose weight, find love, give up cigarettes or drugs, become happy, re-kindle a lost friendship, find yourself, but **it takes a single thought and motivation to make it happen**. That's all it takes, and we know that. People are scared of change, and as intelligent analytical beings we fear so much. The fear of failing is a huge obstacle for most people trying to reach their dreams and was also the main reason it took me so long to get this book published. Without change we grow stagnant, and without change we fail to challenge our very beings.

When I started writing I had a strong feeling that The Lost Keys would sell thousands of copies and hopefully help people find their own keys to happiness. I could have given up when I received my first rejection letter, but I had the motivation to succeed and to share all this with you. I knew it was my soul purpose, plus I enjoy writing as it reaffirms that my experiences and observations are meaningful. All it took was positive thinking and some free time to do what I knew felt right in my heart.

Find and do what makes **<u>you</u>** truly happy and you will reap the benefits. Happiness is far more important than money (as long as you have a roof over your head of course). Those who have money will tell you the same thing. If you enjoy and love what you do, and if it is what you're meant to be doing, then the money will roll in, have no doubt about it. It is just one more of those unwritten rules of the universe. Motivate yourself and do it for you. Do something that will make you happy, find that spark, find that love you had for life when things were simpler.

Remember when people said, "what do you want to do when you are older"? Well, ask yourself that **now**, and follow the dream. Do it now, make that decision right here that you will change your life for the better whilst learning your life lessons. If you follow your dream, and truly believe it is your soul purpose then you will not only benefit yourself but a vast amount of the population as well. We all have different gifts, and are capable of excelling in different fields.

You can read a book and think, "wow that makes so much sense", then put it down and carry on with your life, hoping that something or someone else will make things better. Or you can read a book, apply the lessons to your life, pass on the information to others, and actually **do** something with it. I really hope you will do the latter.

Here is a list of the most important Lost Keys to finding happiness:

- » Deal with past experiences
- » **Love** yourself and others unconditionally
- » Find & learn lessons from the seemingly negative aspects of your life
- » Find your purpose for being here on Earth, at this moment in time

- » **Everything** is impermanent (temporary)
- » Take time to evaluate what you want from life
- » Simplify your life
- » Have compassion for all living things
- » Maintain a healthy life through exercise and good diet
- » Put things into perspective
- » Think of others less fortunate than yourself
- » Remember we are all in this together, as one
- » Take time to let your mind sleep
- » Take quiet time for yourself, looking inward
- » Listen to your body
- » Listen to the messages from your 'Spirit'
- » Listen to the world and use all **six** senses
- » Fight to stay on top
- » Get out and connect with the beauty of nature
- » Never stop learning and improving yourself
- » Balance Invisible Power in social situations
- » Just think happy thoughts and smile frequently
- » Live in the present, don't worry about the past or untold future
- » Have a little faith that your actions will work out positively
- » Balance is the key to everything in this life
- » Trust in the **ABSOLUTE** power of the mind, and use it

This list will make you so much happier, and is capable of transforming your world for the better, but to have control of your thoughts, emotions and mind, is the ultimate key to happiness.

The Lost Keys will help you in a world complicated by our supersonic evolution. They can open the doors to happiness, enlightenment, and spirituality, but everyone must find their own path. You have started on the yellow brick road so continue as you are, learn quickly, keep your eyes and ears open, and why not have a laugh along the way?

When you start looking for spiritual meaning in your life it also begins looking for you. The knowledge of the Universe will lie down and open her legs for you when you begin to live properly and in-tune. When this happens your thirst for life will be immense. You will understand and appreciate *everything* that happens around and to you. Nothing can affect you or shake you, you are content every minute of every day. Life is good, life is fun, life is exciting, magical, simple and perfect.

It is very difficult to write or even explain what I know and feel within me at this moment in time, but trust me, seeking the Lost Keys to happiness is the most worthwhile thing you will **ever** do on this planet. I am by no means at the end of my spiritual quest, so I cannot begin to imagine what it feels like further down the road, it just keeps on getting better and better, more amazing at each stage. Be sure to share your initial experiences with others as it awakens the sleeping spiritual masters residing within them.

On reflection, perhaps I am a Lightworker as my

Mum once said, a being of some form or description that has chosen to come back to help the inhabitants of Earth, a Lightworker come back to help all of humanity correct its abuse of Planet Earth, to help on a Spiritual level, to awaken what **all** humans have inside of them. But then I think we all have the potential to be Lightworkers. Be prepared to start noticing the biggest shift in global perception the world has ever seen.

*With this in mind, and with the knowledge of everything I have shared in this book – go forward, dare to take that next step into the unknown, know with faith that you are part of something much bigger than you. Go out into the world and feel everything, the good and the bad. Learn from both positive and negative and see the reasons behind everything that happens to you. Breathe it in, absorb everything that gets thrown at you. Use your senses, use your intuition, be the person you want to be, look at the world around you, enjoy the simple pleasures, put things into perspective, love, balance everything, run, smile, dance, be positive, travel, do the things that make you happy, invite nature into your life in some form, look for signs, ask and you will receive, feel the higher power in you, take responsibility, take risks, don't hurt people, help each other. **Live life**.*

Life will not always be easy, it has ups and downs, and it will be one big test. Remember that, and if you can use the Lost Keys to help you on your journey you will find happiness, and you will find purpose. Good luck everyone, you have the knowledge, now the rest is, and always will be up to you.

Acknowledgements

I would like to thank everyone I have met on my journey who has taught me lessons about the world and myself. Individually you may not know what you have taught me, but that is what makes human interaction so special – we never know what we are capable of teaching others, and what they might teach us in return.

You include, but are not limited to; my guide in Nepal, soldier on the helicopter in Iraq, Prime Minister, Wes the Irish leprechaun sent at the right time, Nameless Monk in Burma, Adele, Kelly Clarkson, Dad I have never known, sister Vicki, Air Stewardess's, countless dates, Urban family, X Factor contestants, New Age authors, Enya, HH Dali Lama, amazing work friends from all around the globe, and the list goes on and on.

I am so grateful in particular to my Mum who has always

been there to answer my questions about New Age life and who put me back on *the path*. She is a special lady who has done a remarkable job raising us all single-handily and with limitless amounts of love and time. She is an inspiration not only to me, but the countless people she has helped in her own way over the years. To my loving family, a massive thanks for being so normal! I am so grateful that we are close and have shared so many experiences together (the good and the bad).

Also I would like to thank my sister Fanny who patiently helped me find relevant songs for each chapter, questioned some of my more radical thoughts, and has always been there throughout the 'major five' events of my life. Thanks also to the crack team (Steve, Audua, Jolyon, Fanny, and Chrissy) who assisted me with my modest marketing campaign, you have always had faith and never doubted my dream. And to my boyfriend Jolyon who is a quite simply everything I could wish for in another person and who understands me almost as well as I do. Helen and Jen for proof reading the very first version of this book over five years ago. Thom and Hells I thank you for the thousands of hilarious situations we have shared together over the years, which could easily fill another book, you've been great friends through thick and thin. Leon, for the fun you have brought both in and outside of work! Everyone who helped me launch this – friends with contacts, models, friends of friends, and the list goes on. Jo Parsons for suggesting self-publishing as an option. And finally, to everyone else who is in my life, who probably didn't even know that this side of me existed, you make and complete my happy and fun life!